THE HERO TRAP

THE HERO TRAP

The Leader's Shift from Doing to Designing

BILL FLYNN

Berrett-Koehler
PUBLISHERS

Berrett-Koehler Publishers, Inc.
1333 Broadway, Suite P100
Oakland, CA 94612-1921
(510) 817-2277
bkconnection.com

Ordering Information
Quantity sales. Special discounts are available on quantity purchases by corporations, associations, individuals, and others. For details, please go to bkconnection.com to see our bulk discounts or contact bookorders@bkpub.com for more information.
Textbook exam/desk copies. Please consult the General FAQ at bkconnection.com.
Bookstore orders for trade or textbook use. For print books, please contact Penguin Random House Publisher Services at customerservice@penguinrandomhouse.com. For ebooks, contact your favorite distributor.

Distributed to the US trade and internationally by Penguin Random House Publisher Services.

The authorized representative in the EU for product safety and compliance is
EU Compliance Partner, Pärnu mnt. 139b-14, 11317 Tallinn, Estonia,
www.eucompliancepartner.com, +372 5368 65 02.

Printed in the United States of America

Berrett-Koehler books are printed on long-lasting acid-free paper. When it is available, we choose paper that has been manufactured by environmentally responsible processes. These may include using trees grown in sustainable forests, incorporating recycled paper, minimizing chlorine in bleaching, or recycling the energy produced at the paper mill.

Cataloging-in-Publication Data is on file at the Library of Congress.
Library of Congress Control Number: 2026014078
ISBN 9798890572479 (paperback) | ISBN 9798890572486 (pdf) | ISBN 9798890572493 (epub)

First Edition
35 34 33 32 31 30 29 28 27 26 10 9 8 7 6 5 4 3 2 1

Book production: Happenstance Type-O-Rama
Cover design: Ashley Ingram

For Maggie—the finest human being I know

CONTENTS

FOREWORD

Bill Flynn names a problem most leaders feel but rarely articulate: the moment when being good at solving problems quietly turns you into the problem. *The Hero Trap* captures that shift with clarity and honesty, showing how success can harden into dependency—and why working harder only tightens the trap. This book doesn't shame the hero; it explains how heroes are made, rewarded, and then exhausted by the very systems they helped build.

What makes this work stand out is how practical it is. Flynn doesn't argue for "letting go" in the abstract. He shows how leaders can redesign the system so they no longer have to be everywhere, decide everything, or save the day at 3:17 a.m. The move from hands-on control to intentional design is framed not as a personality change, but as a leadership evolution that matches the complexity of modern organizations.

The writing is grounded, human, and deeply relatable. You see yourself in the late-night Slack messages, the invisible dependencies, the quiet realization that your organization only works when you're in the room. Flynn makes it clear that this isn't a failure of character or effort—it's a predictable outcome of success in environments that outgrow individual capacity.

The Hero Trap is a guide for leaders ready to stop being the bottleneck and start building something that lasts. It's about keeping your eyes on what matters, taking your hands off what shouldn't require you, and creating organizations that run on purpose instead of personality. If you're tired of being indispensable—and ready to be effective—this book will meet you exactly where you are.

—Dr. Marshall Goldsmith is the *Thinkers50* #1 Executive Coach and *New York Times* bestselling author of *The Earned Life*, *Triggers*, and *What Got You Here Won't Get You There*.

INTRODUCTION

The Identity Crisis Every Successful Leader Faces

It was 3:17 a.m. when Alex Chen finally admitted he was drowning. He'd been staring at his laptop for hours—crisis emails, two customer escalations, and a road map that made no sense because sales had promised the impossible.

Another Slack ping: "Alex, quick call? Client is threatening to cancel."

He typed, "Give me ten minutes," then stared out the window.

When did this happen? When did I become . . . this? And if I stopped—would any of it hold?

The irony wasn't lost on him. Three years ago, he'd left his corporate job specifically to build something different. A company where people could do their best work without the politics and bottlenecks that had frustrated him for years. Now he'd become the biggest bottleneck of all.

His wife, Emma, had stopped asking when he'd be home.

But last Tuesday, she'd said something worse.

Alex had been on his laptop at the kitchen table—just checking one thread, he'd promised—when Emma appeared in the doorway. Not angry. That would have been easier. Just tired in a way that had nothing to do with sleep.

"Sophie asked me today why you look at your phone during dinner."

Alex's fingers froze. "I don't—I put it face down—"

"You put it face down. You still check it every time it buzzes." Emma leaned against the doorframe. "She notices, Alex. She asked me if your phone is more important than we are."

"What did you say?"

"I didn't know what to say." She paused. "I used to know."

She went back to bed. Alex sat there, hand still on the keyboard, Marcus's question about the pricing model glowing on the screen—his head of sales always had one more thing. His thumb hovered over the phone.

He typed the response anyway.

That was the moment he couldn't unknow. Not the 3:17 a.m. crisis—those felt heroic, necessary, justified. This was just a Tuesday. Just dinner. Just his daughter learning that Dad's attention was always borrowed, never owned.

His team, brilliant people he'd personally recruited, were starting to look elsewhere. And the mission that had driven him to start ParagonCX—helping other companies solve their customer experience problems—was getting lost in the chaos of his own operational dysfunction.

The Hero Trap

Most leaders don't fall into the Hero Trap because they're control freaks. They fall in because they care too much to watch things break, at least at first.

You were rewarded for saving the day—again and again. Decisive. Relentless. Dependable. Sharp. The irony is that those same traits built a system that now depends on you to survive. The more competent you became, the more the organization quietly organized itself around you.

You didn't design a dependency out of ego; you inherited it through success. And you keep inheriting it.

You tell yourself it's just this once. The stakes are too high. You'll step back after this crisis passes.

But the crisis passes, and another one arrives, and somehow you're back in the room making the calls. The ones you swore you wouldn't make anymore. Not because the team can't handle it. But because stepping back in feels responsible.

> **Pressure doesn't change who you are. It *reveals* who you are.**

This isn't a story about becoming someone else overnight. It's about learning where—and how—to stop being the bottleneck first.

In working with hundreds of leaders across industries as a coach, executive, consultant, speaker, adviser, and mentor, I've observed a consistent pattern: Almost all start as Controllers. Not because they're control freaks—many have no choice. Their organizations have been built around their personal capacity, and stepping back would mean watching things break.

Some remain Controllers because circumstances demand it. Others because the identity shift feels like too great a loss. A few make the transition to Builder—learning to develop others and create frameworks that extend beyond themselves. Fewer still become true Architects, designing systems that generate solutions they never imagined.

And here's what surprised me most: The leaders who achieve Architect thinking rarely transform wholesale. They become Architects in specific domains first—delegation, or cross-functional coordination, or strategic patience—while remaining Builders or even Controllers in others. The progression is uneven, sometimes frustratingly so. But it's real, and it's learnable.

That's what this book is designed to help you do.

The Hero Trap follows a predictable arc: success that begins as personal excellence, scales into control, and ends as constraint.

By the time Alex realized he was the system, not just inside it, he was already exhausted.

Alex is a composite drawn from my own experience, my clients, and the research behind this book.

He is a founder CEO, so the trap is easy to see. But it doesn't start or end there.

It starts with the department head who reviews every deliverable. The VP who answers every question before the room has time to think. The new manager still fixing the team's work late at night.

Different roles. Same experience.

If you've ever felt indispensable and exhausted in the same breath, this book is about you.

Alex didn't wake up one morning and decide to micromanage ParagonCX into stagnation. It happened one crisis at a time—one late-night save, one "let me just handle it" moment. Every success reinforced the same invisible rule: When Alex steps in, things get better.

Until one day, they didn't.

Alex's crisis isn't unique. Every system of rewards—from childhood gold stars to executive bonuses—trains leaders to be indispensable problem solvers. That identity creates short-term success but long-term fragility.

The paradox: The more problems you solve personally, the more dependent your company becomes on you. The more dependent it becomes, the more fragile it gets. And the more fragile it gets, the harder it is to stop being the hero.

If you've ever found yourself working harder as your team grows larger, if success seems to demand more of you instead of less, you're already in the Hero Trap.

This book is about what happens next. How leaders like Alex, and perhaps you, learn to step out of the spotlight, redesign the system, and build organizations that are guided by purpose instead of personality.

Before you read further, try one thing. On a scale of one to ten, how confident are you that your current approach to leadership will still work when your organization is twice as complex as it is today?

Most leaders say seven or eight. Not ten—they're too honest for that. But high enough to keep doing what they're doing.

Now ask yourself: *Why not nine?*

Whatever just surfaced—that's worth paying attention to. Not because I have the answer. But because you already have the doubt. This book helps you do something with it.

But why is the Hero Trap so much more powerful now than it was for previous generations of leaders? Alex's crisis wasn't just personal—it was symptomatic of three converging forces that make traditional leadership exponentially more difficult than it was even in the early 2020s.

For Alex, those forces weren't abstract. They were already tightening around him at 3:17 a.m.—success patterns that rewarded his answers, an environment changing faster than he could plan, and a growing web of interdependencies that no one person could manage. What felt like exhaustion was really friction between an old identity built on control and a new reality demanding design.

The Three Invisible Forces Making Leadership Exponentially Harder

These are structural pressures built into how organizations grow, how environments shift, and how the success patterns that made you effective gradually work against the system you're trying to lead.

Force 1: Success Patterns Working Against You

Recognition check: Does your individual excellence now constrain your organization's growth?

Every system that rewarded you for having answers now punishes your organization for depending on you. The promotion patterns that advanced you, the performance reviews that rated you, the cultural narratives that named you "high potential," all were designed for a world where leaders could personally manage complexity. That world no longer exists.

Your education taught you to be the smartest person in the room. Your early career rewarded you for solving problems others couldn't. Your leadership promotions came because you delivered exceptional individual results. But individual capacity scales linearly, while organizational complexity scales exponentially.

Force 2: The BANI Environment

Recognition check: Are you trying to control situations that require adaptation instead?

We've moved from VUCA (volatile, uncertain, complex, ambiguous) to what futurist Jamais Cascio calls BANI conditions—brittle, anxious, nonlinear, incomprehensible.[1] Your training taught you to manage through planning and control. BANI conditions require sensing and adapting through systems that can evolve faster than you can think.

Markets shift overnight. Customer expectations change mid-project. Technology capabilities leap forward unpredictably. The strategic planning cycles that worked when change was quarterly now break when change is daily.

Force 3: Systems Complexity Explosion

Recognition check: Do you find yourself overwhelmed by interdependencies you can't track?

The number of potential connections in your organization grows exponentially, not linearly (see figure 1). A team of five has ten possible relationships. A team of fifty has 1,225. Your brain wasn't designed to manage exponential complexity through individual effort, but your systems can be.

Every new tool, process, stakeholder, or market relationship multiplies the combinations you need to consider. What worked when you could personally track all the moving pieces fails when the number of moving pieces exceeds your cognitive capacity.

The Invisible Explosion

Consider what "handling a customer complaint" actually means now versus what it meant when most of today's leaders learned their craft.

A generation ago, a frustrated customer called your support line. One person answered, checked the order in one system, maybe consulted

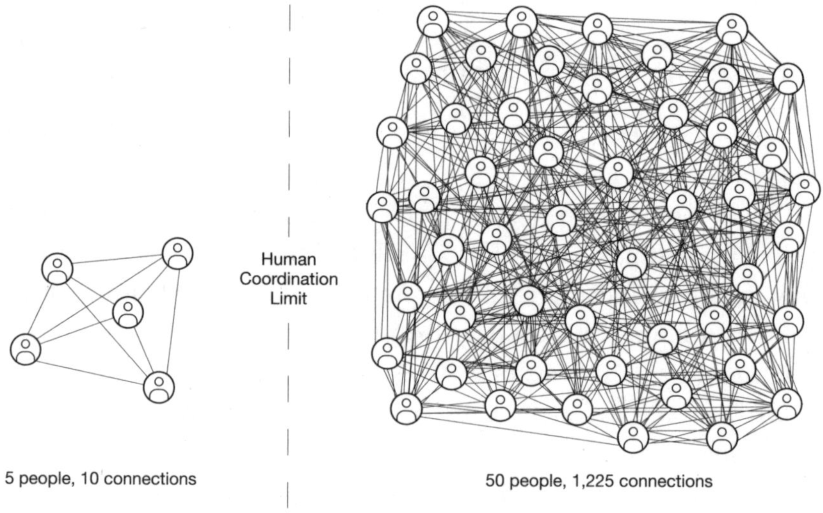

FIGURE 1. *The Complexity Explosion.* Five people, ten connections. Fifty people, 1,225. Your brain can't track exponential growth. Your systems can.

a manager, and resolved the issue. Three people, two systems, fifteen minutes.

Now that same complaint triggers a cascade no one person can track. The customer posts on social media (monitored by marketing). They email support (routed through an AI triage system to a specialist team). They dispute the charge with their bank (flagged by finance, escalated to legal). Meanwhile, the CRM logs the interaction, the product team receives an automated sentiment alert, customer success checks the account health score, and sales sees the renewal risk flag.

One complaint. Twelve systems. Eight teams. Forty-seven potential handoff points where something can break.

This didn't happen overnight. It accumulated gradually—one integration, one tool, one process at a time—until leaders found themselves accountable for webs of interdependency that exceed what any human brain can hold. Most can't draw their own organization's information flow on a whiteboard anymore. The complexity crept in while everyone was busy being productive.

This isn't a new problem. It's an invisible one—a condition you've been operating under for years without a name for it. And it's accelerating. External forces keep adding complexity from outside (new regulations, market shifts, technology changes), while your own heroic leadership keeps adding complexity from inside.

This is what "incomprehensible" actually means in BANI conditions. It's not that the world recently became confusing. It's that the systems inside your own organization crossed the threshold of individual comprehension years ago—and the gap between what you can hold in your head and what you're accountable for widens every quarter.

Alex experienced this at ParagonCX without recognizing it. Every system he added to "improve efficiency"—the CRM, the project management tool, the customer health dashboard, the automated alerts—created new connection points. Each connection created new failure modes. Each failure mode created new demands on his attention. He thought he was building capability. He was manufacturing complexity.

Worse, every time Alex "saved the day," he added invisible threads to the web. The heroic fix that bypassed the normal process. The exception he approved because it was faster. The decision he made because explaining it would take too long. Each intervention created dependencies that only he could manage—dependencies no one documented because they lived in Alex's head.

> **The hero doesn't just fail to manage complexity. The hero generates it.**

To surface the hidden complexity you've built or inherited—the invisible threads, undocumented dependencies, and heroic workarounds that now require your constant attention—see the Complexity Debt Audit in appendix I (access the appendices at catalystgrowthadvisors.com/the-hero-trap/*).*

The math confirms what your gut already knows. When you add one new system to an environment with ten existing systems, you don't add one connection—you add ten. Add a twelfth system, you add eleven more. This is why organizations feel exponentially harder to lead even when head count grows linearly. It's also why working harder can't solve the problem—the complexity grows faster than your capacity to process it.

And here's what makes this especially dangerous: Research on the "illusion of explanatory depth" shows that people systematically overestimate how well they understand complex systems. Ask someone to explain how a toilet works, and they'll confidently begin—then falter when pressed for details.[2] The same pattern applies to organizational systems. Leaders mistake familiarity for comprehension, activity for mastery. They believe they understand their organizations far better than they actually do.

The Integration Challenge

These three invisible forces don't just coexist—they compound each other. Success patterns make you resist change precisely when BANI conditions demand adaptation. Systems complexity overwhelms individual capacity exactly when traditional leadership approaches hit their limits. And every heroic intervention that "works" reinforces the success patterns that keep you trapped.

Most leaders respond by working harder, staying later, or trying to become better heroes. But that's like trying to outrun a flood by running faster. The water rises quicker than your legs can move.

The counterintuitive truth: These same forces that destroy hero-dependent organizations create competitive moats for Architect-designed systems.

Complexity breaks the leader who tries to hold it all in their head. But complexity becomes an asset when you design systems that navigate it without requiring your constant attention. The organization that builds those systems can handle what competitors cannot—not because its leaders are smarter, but because its architecture is better.

Example: The Product Launch Bottleneck

In growing organizations, complexity first shows up at the seams, especially during launches. Early on, a single leader can coordinate every moving part and catch problems before customers ever notice. But as the number of launches multiplies, that same control becomes the bottleneck.

The Architect leader responds by building a launch system with shared milestones, defined roles, decision rights, and real-time visibility. Suddenly, the company can run five launches with half the drama of one.

The same complexity that once demanded a hero now rewards an Architect.

The solution isn't becoming a better hero. It's recognizing that heroic leadership has a ceiling—and you've hit it. The path forward is evolving from hero to Architect through intentional identity development.

The Three Leadership Identities: Your Strategic Response

Understanding these three forces explains why the Hero Trap feels so inescapable—but it also reveals the path forward. The way out isn't eliminating your expertise or working harder. It's developing the capability to choose your leadership identity strategically based on what each situation requires.

Depending on the situation, leaders tend to shift among three modes: Controller, Builder, and Architect. Together, these form the *CBA model*—a shorthand you'll see throughout this book to describe the leadership ROI that comes from shifting your identity (see figure 2):

CBA MODEL

- **Controller:** "I solve." Direct action when crisis demands immediate intervention or technical expertise is required.
- **Builder:** "I show how I solve." Systematic capability development when coaching and framework building will scale impact.
- **Architect:** "I design systems that solve." Structural design when you need capability that works independently of your involvement.

Consider a sales leader. As a Controller, you close every deal yourself. As a Builder, you teach your method. However, when the customer goes off script (and they always do), the team comes back to you again and again. As an Architect, you design a playbook with decision rules, so the team handles exceptions using the judgment you embedded into the system.

Builder scales your effort. Architect scales your judgment.

The key insight: Sometimes Controller is exactly right—in a genuine crisis, when technical expertise is required, or when immediate action prevents larger problems. Sometimes Builder is optimal—when developing people's capabilities will create lasting change. Sometimes Architect is essential—when you need systems that work without heroic intervention.

That's why I frame these identities together as the CBA model: not to replace your identity, but to expand your repertoire as a leader.

Development progression:

Controller excellence ➔ Builder development ➔ Architect capability

Key capabilities you'll develop:

- recognition (reading what this situation needs)
- repertoire (operating effectively from choice rather than default)

Most leaders bounce between these identities unconsciously, defaulting to Controller under pressure. The question that defines your legacy

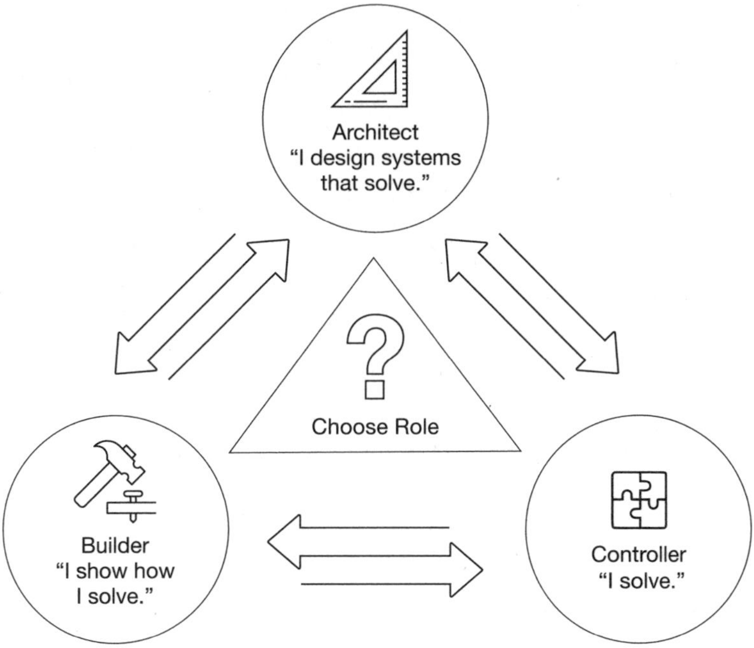

FIGURE 2. *The CBA Model.* Controller: "I solve." Builder: "I show how I solve." Architect: "I design systems that solve." The question isn't which identity is best. It's which one this moment requires.

is this: In your highest-leverage situations, can you choose your leadership identity strategically, or do you default to whatever made you successful before?

Important: Your Leadership Choice Point

By the end of this book, you'll have a clear framework for choosing your leadership identity strategically based on what your organization needs, not just what feels familiar.

Take a moment to consider: If you could choose your leadership identity based on what your organization needs rather than defaulting to what made you successful individually, what would that make possible for you personally? For your team? For your organization?

Write that down. That's your "why" for the transformation ahead.

Your Leadership Identity Snapshot

Before you turn the page, pause for a quick check-in. Which identity best describes how you currently operate?

PROBLEM-SOLVING IDENTITY

✓ **Controller:** I personally dive in when complex problems arise.

✓ **Builder:** I work with others, building their capabilities.

✓ **Architect:** I focus on preventing problems through better systems.

DECISION-MAKING IDENTITY

✓ **Controller:** I make most strategic calls myself.

✓ **Builder:** I guide outcomes by including others in the process.

✓ **Architect:** I ensure our systems generate good choices without me.

TEAM-LEADERSHIP IDENTITY

✓ **Controller:** I manage through oversight and intervention.

✓ **Builder:** I grow people and improve processes.

✓ **Architect:** I design structures that develop collective capability.

Where do you see yourself defaulting? These answers mark the starting point of your leadership identity journey.

Why This Is Hard

Shifting from hero to Architect isn't just about skills. It's about identity.

The hero identity wasn't installed when you became a leader. It was being assembled your entire life—by the school systems that rewarded individual answers, the career paths that promoted problem solvers, and the neurological patterns that formed long before your first management role. It formed not from ego but from usefulness, and for a long time, it worked. That's why willpower fails. You're not fighting a habit. You're fighting decades of reinforcement. Which is exactly why you need systems, not determination.

But under pressure, especially financial pressure, leaders often default to Controller mode.

Culture reinforces it, systems reward it, and identity clings to it. And here's what most leaders don't anticipate: The organization resists too. Teams trained to depend on a hero don't feel empowered when the hero steps back. They feel abandoned. Their instincts have atrophied, not because they lost capability, but because the system taught them not to use it. The leader who tries to change too quickly faces pressure from more than one direction: their own habits pulling them back in, and a team that hasn't yet learned to trust itself again. That's why the Hero Trap is so sticky: It's a design problem on both sides.

Most leaders can recognize this privately. Imagine stepping away for a full month with no emergency access—not checking messages, not quietly monitoring, not acting as the final backstop. Would the organization continue improving, or would decisions slow while people waited? The hesitation many leaders feel at that question is not ego. It is responsibility, and it reveals how much of your organization's coordination currently lives inside your head.

The payoff for Architect work shows up in seasons, not sprints. That gap is maddening. When you can't see results this week, your brain nudges you back toward what always worked: Solve something, feel useful, move on. This is the identity lock-in we described earlier: Your brain is getting rewarded for the very behaviors that limit your organization's growth.

Early in the transition, results often worsen briefly. Decisions take longer, more questions surface, and small mistakes appear. Leaders usually interpret this as proof they stepped back too soon. In reality, it is evidence the organization is relearning how to think without immediate intervention. If the leader reenters quickly, stability returns but dependence strengthens; if the boundary holds, capability develops.

That reward cycle does something else, too. It protects the mental model that justifies the behavior.

Psychologists call this *assimilation*—absorbing new information into your existing mental model without changing the model itself. A leader who reads a book about delegation and thinks, "Great, now I'm a hero who delegates better," is assimilating. The technique gets absorbed; the identity stays untouched. The opposite process is *accommodation*—recognizing that your model itself needs to change. That's harder. It means sitting with the discomfort of not knowing who you are as a leader if you're not the one solving problems.

Most leadership development fails because it gets assimilated. Leaders add new techniques to an unchanged identity. This book asks for accommodation. That's why parts of it will feel uncomfortable in ways that other leadership books don't. You're not adding tools to the hero model. You're redesigning the model.

You may have seen this already. A new operating cadence, clearer decision rights, a delegation push, or a leadership framework works for a few weeks. Then exceptions accumulate, people check "just to be safe," and the leader steps in once to prevent a mistake. Within months, the system has reorganized around the same center again. The problem was not commitment. The system absorbed the change while the underlying model stayed intact.

That's why identity work alone isn't enough—without redesigning the system around you, the old model reasserts itself. The problem was never effort or intention. It was structure.

A note on charisma: This book isn't an argument against inspiration, vision, or personal magnetism. Alan Mulally transformed Ford not by suppressing his warmth but by channeling it into systems. Bob Chapman built Barry-Wehmiller's culture through genuine care—systematized into daily practices. The most magnetic leaders I've worked with didn't abandon their presence. They designed structures that extended their impact beyond the room they happened to be in.

The Hero Trap isn't about personality type. Power players, creative communicators, analytical backend leaders—all can fall into it, and all can escape it. What varies is the starting point, not the destination.

None of this means the hero behavior was wrong. In earlier stages of growth, it was often the most responsible action available. The difficulty is not that the leader failed to adapt; it is that the organization outgrew a coordination method that once worked.

Design Beats Default

The way out isn't trying harder. It's designing systems—decision rights, information flows, recognition patterns—that align behavior with your chosen identity. Without them, Controller mode wins every time.

W. Edwards Deming argued that 94 percent of problems are system problems—not people problems. Most leaders eventually absorb that lesson. But software architect Ruth Malan identified a deeper layer: "If the architecture of the system and the architecture of the organization are at odds, the architecture of the organization wins."[3]

That's the Architect's real work—not designing better processes, but designing the organizational architecture that makes better processes inevitable: the decision rights, information flows, team structures, and incentive patterns that shape behavior even when you're not in the room.

Architects don't just declare their identity. They build organizations that express it.

Leaders try to change behavior through reminders and effort. Architecture changes behavior by making the desired action the easiest action.

The Signal Box

Key insights from this chapter:

- Heroics feel productive but create dependency.
- Architecting systems feels slower but builds lasting capability.
- The goal isn't to build systems—it's to build systems that *work when you're not there.*

Learning Prompt

Where does your organization currently depend on you? This week, design one small system that lets the work happen excellently without you. The test: Can it still function when you're on vacation?

Segue to Alex's Journey

Alex was about to discover a hard truth: Organizations don't change because leaders push harder; they change when leaders rewire the system itself. His next moves would decide whether he stayed trapped as the indispensable hero or became the kind of Architect whose organization could thrive without him. Most leaders never make that shift. Alex's story shows why.

HOW TO USE THIS BOOK (AND WHY IT'S BUILT THIS WAY)

You don't have to read *The Hero Trap* cover to cover to benefit from it. That's not an accident. It's a design choice. Most leadership books assume a single kind of reader and a single kind of reading experience: Start at page one, move straight through, absorb the ideas, then figure out how to apply them later. But real leaders don't read that way. They are capable, well intentioned, and overloaded. They reach for the book when something breaks. They come back when the next challenge hits.

I tried to write a different kind of leadership book, one that honors both the reader and the leader.

This book assumes you are not broken, behind, or failing at leadership. It assumes you inherited systems that quietly organized themselves around your competence, and that those systems now limit scale. Rather than blaming individuals, the book focuses on redesign. Rather than forcing a single reading path, it offers multiple ways in, so you can engage at the depth your reality allows.

Multiple Paths Through the Book

You can use *The Hero Trap* in whatever way fits your needs right now:

- **The Fast Track:** In thirty to sixty minutes, you'll see the core Controller–Builder–Architect (CBA) framework, complete a quick assessment, and identify the few "moves that matter" to begin shifting from heroic leadership to architectural leadership immediately.

- **The Main Journey:** Follow the story of Alex Chen and ParagonCX chapter by chapter. Each turning point unpacks a critical shift from Controller ➔ Builder ➔ Architect, blending lived experience with practical frameworks you can apply in your own context.
- **The Signal Box:** At the end of each chapter, this section distills what matters most—the signal versus the noise. If you're short on time or revisiting the book later, these summaries capture the essential insights without requiring a full reread.
- **Behavioral/Quality Science Boxes:** Scattered throughout the chapters, these optional sections or Behavioral/Quality Science Boxes explain *why* the concepts work. They draw on established research in decision science, systems thinking, motivation, quality, and psychology. Skip them if you want a purely practical path; read them if you want to understand the underlying mechanisms that drive behavior and performance.
- **Learning Prompts:** Each chapter ends with reflection prompts designed to help you pause, think, and apply the ideas directly to your own leadership environment. These are not abstract questions; they are meant to surface design choices you can act on.
- **Tool Kit and Appendices:** For evidence-driven leaders and L&D practitioners, these resources include assessments, templates, and references to help embed architectural leadership into real systems, not just personal habits (access these resources at *catalystgrowthadvisors.com/the-hero-trap/*).

Why This Structure Matters

For decades, leadership research has focused on optimizing leaders—their traits, behaviors, and styles—while treating followership as a given. I believe that they have been studying the wrong hand. This book starts earlier. It asks why people would choose to commit in the first place, and treats membership—ownership, autonomy, and safety to act—as the designable variable that makes heroic leadership unnecessary.

The structure of the book mirrors that belief. Instead of asking you to adapt to the book, the book adapts to how leaders actually learn, decide, and apply ideas under pressure—layered so time-pressed readers get immediate value, while deeper learners get the behavioral science behind every framework.

Whether you move quickly, immerse yourself in the full story, or work directly with the tools, the goal is the same: to help you escape the Hero Trap and shift from heroic leadership to architectural leadership—designing systems that outperform any single leader, including you.

Research Integrity Note

All performance claims reflect ranges observed in documented case studies and implementation experiences rather than guaranteed outcomes. Results vary based on implementation quality, organizational context, leadership commitment, and environmental factors. This work prioritizes practical application while maintaining grounding in established academic and business research.

Some case examples and outcome descriptions reflect commonly cited accounts in the literature and practitioner sources. Exact metrics and phrasing may vary by source and are intended to illustrate patterns rather than serve as formal case documentation.

Composite Scenarios

All company stories and characters (e.g., ParagonCX and Alex Chen) are composites built from real experiences and research to illustrate full transformations that no single example captures completely. These are intentionally fictionalized to protect confidentiality and to show the complete arc from heroic leadership to architectural design.

Methodology and Framework Development

The Controller–Builder–Architect framework, Push–Pull–Habit–Anxiety model, and Performance Operating System are original constructs developed by the author, synthesized from decades of research and practice across leadership, operations, behavioral science, and systems theory.

Acknowledgment of Integration

While every effort has been made to cite direct influences and specific frameworks, the ideas in this book represent a synthesis of countless conversations, observations, and learnings from leaders, researchers, and practitioners who have dedicated their careers to understanding how organizations and leadership can become more effective and sustainable.

The frameworks and methodologies presented have been tested and refined through executive coaching, consulting projects, workshops, and training programs delivered to thousands of leaders across industries. The integration of systems thinking, followership research, decision science, and organizational psychology into a coherent leadership transformation methodology represents the collective wisdom of the many thinkers and practitioners whose work is cited here.

About the Performance Operating System Series

This book is the foundation. It addresses what comes first: the leadership identity transformation from Controller to Builder to Architect that makes all systematic improvement possible.

Future books in this series apply that framework to specific operational domains—strategy execution, decision-making, team design, and financial operations. Each stands alone; together they form a complete Performance Operating System.

If you want more now, *Further, Faster* (2020) introduced some of these concepts in an earlier form. The volumes ahead will develop them fully.

For current availability, tools, and resources, go to *catalystgrowthadvisors.com/catalyst-growth-advisors/the-hero-trap-book/*.

PART I

DEEPER: ESCAPING THE CONTROLLER MINDSET

THE FIRST DIMENSION OF ARCHITECTURAL leadership is the hardest to begin: seeing the trap you helped build. This requires diagnosis over action, addressing root causes over surface fixes, designing for ownership over earning loyalty, and recognizing that the strengths that got you here are now what hold you back. When you master the "deeper" dimension, you stop solving problems and start seeing the systems that produce them.

- **WHERE YOU ARE: Trapped in your own success. The skills that made you exceptional—solving problems, having answers, being indispensable—now constrain your organization's growth.**
- **WHERE YOU'RE GOING: From solving problems to seeing systems. From being the answer to designing how answers emerge.**
- **CHAPTERS 1–4 help you recognize the Hero Trap, think in systems, understand why followership backfires, and design for ownership.**
- **YOU'RE READY FOR PART II WHEN: You catch yourself asking "What system would prevent this?" instead of "How do I fix this?"**

CHAPTER 1

Great to Good

The Hero's Success Paradox

***Heroes carry organizations on their backs.
Architects build organizations that carry themselves.***

Alex Chen's 3:17 a.m. crisis, described in the introduction, wasn't unique. Across industries, in organizations of every size, successful leaders are discovering the same devastating truth: The very capabilities that made them valuable are systematically destroying their organizations' ability to succeed without them.

At ParagonCX, Alex had built the company from fifteen to fifty employees through sheer brilliance. His heroic leadership had earned him industry recognition, investor praise, and a company valued at $80 million. Their AI-powered customer success platform helped mid-market SaaS companies predict and prevent churn with remarkable accuracy.

Most nights ended the same way—Slack threads multiplying faster than he could answer, unread emails blinking like warning lights. Emma would fall asleep beside the glow of his laptop while Alex typed one more reply, convinced it would buy him peace tomorrow. Instead, the requests always returned, louder and more urgent. The more he fixed, the more everyone waited for him to fix. Competence had slowly, imperceptibly become captivity.

> **Success carried a hidden cost.**

Alex didn't see it coming. A week after the board praised Paragon-CX's latest quarter—revenue up 40 percent, churn down, three enterprise deals in the pipeline—he walked into a product review feeling, for the first time in months, like the machine was running.

Six people around the table. Alex opened with the integration architecture for the Meridian account—a problem he'd been turning over for days. He laid out the approach, walked through the trade-offs, asked if anyone saw gaps.

Silence.

Not the silence of agreement. The silence of people who'd stopped trying.

He looked at Priya, his senior engineer—the one he'd recruited personally from Google, the one whose systems thinking had impressed him more than anyone else's in the interview process. She was looking at her laptop. Not typing. Just looking at it.

"Priya—what do you think about the API layer? You've built more of these than anyone here."

She glanced up. "It's fine."

"Fine?"

"It's good, Alex. It'll work."

He knew it wasn't her best thinking. He'd seen her best thinking—it was sharper than his, more elegant, three steps ahead. But she offered "fine" the way you hand a form back to someone who's already filled it out.

After the meeting, he caught her in the hallway. "That wasn't your real opinion in there."

Priya stopped. She chose her next words carefully.

"I stopped pushing for better solutions a while ago. In the end, you always decide anyway." She paused. "It's not a criticism, Alex. You're usually right. But being right isn't the same thing as building a team that thinks."

She said it gently. That made it worse.

He stood in the hallway after she walked away, his hand still on the doorframe. The exit interviews from three departing engineers suddenly made sense. People weren't leaving the mission or the opportunity—they were leaving because they'd learned their thinking didn't matter.

The tragedy wasn't a lack of talent—it was that capable people had learned not to use it. And Alex had taught them. Not through malice or neglect, but through sheer competence. Every answer he gave was a question someone else stopped asking.

His heroic leadership had created learned helplessness at scale.

But Alex's story reveals something crucial about leadership transformation: Recognizing the problem is only the beginning. The real challenge lies in understanding why intelligent, well-intentioned leaders get trapped in heroic patterns and what it takes to escape.

In appendix II ("Architect Systems in Practice"), you'll see how seven organizations, from Amazon to Zingerman's, escaped this same trap by replacing personal heroics with system design. Each turned leadership intent into structure so that progress no longer depended on a single "Alex." (Access the appendices at *catalystgrowthadvisors.com/the-hero-trap/*.)

Leadership Experts Have Been Studying the Wrong Hand

When we applaud, both hands matter equally, but traditional leadership development focuses entirely on the leader's actions while ignoring the follower's experience. You'd develop elaborate theories about hand positioning, finger coordination, and palm acoustics, all while ignoring that applause requires *two hands working together*.

For decades, leadership research has obsessed over what makes leaders effective—their decision-making styles, communication techniques, emotional intelligence, strategic thinking. Meanwhile, the fundamental question has been ignored: *Why do people choose to follow?*

This is exactly what we've done with leadership. We've obsessed over the "leader hand"—their charisma, vision, and decision-making—while treating followership as a given. But as leadership researchers Robert

Hogan, Robert Kaiser, and Mark van Vugt point out, focusing on leadership alone is like trying to understand clapping by studying only the left hand.[1]

The Real Puzzle

Why do people follow?

It's obvious why people want to lead—power, status, influence, the ability to shape outcomes. The puzzle is why anyone would willingly surrender autonomy to someone else. Why would rational individuals give up control over their time, decisions, and resources to follow another person's vision?

Marcus Buckingham, former Gallup researcher and coauthor of *Nine Lies About Work*, cuts straight to the heart of this mystery: "Leadership isn't a thing, because it cannot be measured reliably. Followership is a thing, because it can."[2] This insight reframes the entire conversation. For decades, we've tried to decode an unmeasurable phenomenon—leadership traits—while overlooking a measurable one: followership outcomes. It's like trying to understand music by studying only the composer while ignoring whether anyone listens.

But understanding why people follow reveals something uncomfortable: Most of what we call "leadership" creates resistance, not engagement.

Captain David Marquet discovered this the hard way on the USS *Santa Fe*—and what he found was that followership isn't the boring hand. It's the more mysterious one.

The USS *Santa Fe*: When Heroes Create Disasters

Captain David Marquet was in trouble before he even stepped aboard the USS *Santa Fe*.

For months, he had prepared to command the USS *Olympia*, studying every system, memorizing every procedure. This was the heroic leadership model he'd been taught: The captain must know more than anyone else on the submarine.

Then, weeks before taking command, the navy reassigned him to the *Santa Fe*—a completely different class of submarine with different systems and capabilities. He would have to command a nuclear submarine he barely understood, with a crew that knew the boat far better than he did.

It was 1999, and the *Santa Fe* was the worst-performing submarine in the Pacific Fleet. Morale was devastated, retention was abysmal, and the crew had developed a culture of learned helplessness.

During a routine drill, Marquet's lack of submarine-specific knowledge created a dangerous moment. He gave what he thought was a standard order: "All ahead two-thirds."

His officer repeated the command with crisp military precision: "All ahead two-thirds, aye sir."

The helmsman hesitated, looking troubled, but prepared to comply.

Something in that hesitation made Marquet pause. "What's wrong?"

"Sir, there is no 'two-thirds' setting on electric propulsion."

Marquet had given an impossible order. But his officer had repeated it anyway, and the helmsman was preparing to attempt something that couldn't be done, simply because the captain had commanded it. In a nuclear submarine where a single mistake can be catastrophic, this heroic leadership model wasn't just inefficient—it was potentially deadly.

That realization triggered a radical decision that violated everything Marquet had been taught about command: Instead of perfecting control, he would give it away.

Marquet's insight wasn't about charisma or courage; it was about *architecture*. By moving authority to where the information lived, he rewired the system. He stopped giving orders and started asking questions. He replaced answers with frameworks. He moved from controlling decisions to designing systems that enabled better ones.

Most leaders think empowerment is about motivation. Marquet proved it's about *mechanics*. He didn't tell people to "own it." He redesigned how ownership worked.

Why it matters: Every leader faces the same inflection point. You can scale yourself. Or, you can scale your system. The first path creates speed and control; the second creates capacity and trust. Marquet's transformation wasn't an act of genius; it was a deliberate redesign of how work happened. His success wasn't that he made people bolder. It's that he made the *system safer* for boldness.

The results for the *Santa Fe*, according to Marquet, were unprecedented:[3]

- went from worst to first in the entire fleet
- achieved the highest retention and operational standings in the navy
- continued winning awards and setting records long after he left command
- produced ten submarine captains over the following decade—more than any other submarine in the fleet

The insight that revolutionized naval leadership: Your value as a leader isn't what you do—it's what you design others to accomplish without you.

But this wasn't just a military breakthrough. The same transformation from heroic leadership to architectural thinking applies across every industry, every size of organization, every level of complexity.

When decisions stall on your team, what are people waiting for—information, permission, or courage? Each answer points to a design flaw, not a talent gap.

What Marquet achieved under the ocean is what every leader must learn on land: Scaling requires architecture, not heroics. And the same dynamic was unfolding at ParagonCX.

ParagonCX: The Hidden Cost of Heroic Success

Back at ParagonCX, Alex Chen's crisis haunted every growth-stage leader who's ever wondered if their early success might become their downfall.

In leadership meetings, Alex caught himself answering every question before anyone else had a chance to speak. Marketing raised a churn concern; he offered three fixes. The room went quiet. Later, his COO told him privately, "The team has ideas, but they don't share them because you always jump in first." He wasn't just solving problems. He was unintentionally shutting down the very people he'd hired for their expertise.

That night, he voiced it to Maya, VP of product: "I'm in every major decision. I solve more problems than ever, but we're moving slower than when we were half this size."

What once made him indispensable was now holding the company back. His greatest strengths were becoming the organization's constraints.

As we learned in the introduction, Alex had become trapped in Controller mode. The crisis was forcing him to acknowledge his two unchosen paths: the Builder path of teaching, and the Architect path of systematic design.

The hero becomes the Controller when success turns into obligation. What began as initiative becomes identity, and once identity fuses with the system, stepping back doesn't just risk failure. It feels like self-erasure.

As described in the Hero Trap, the same instincts that built your reputation now bind your organization's capacity.

You can see the signs everywhere: dependence on your decisions, growth that slows as the team expands, exhaustion disguised as dedication. Each one signals a deeper problem. The system's design revolves around your presence.

That's when the real transformation begins: shifting from Controller to Builder to Architect.

Every leader operates somewhere along this progression—from Controller, who solves directly, to Architect, who designs systems that solve. Understanding where you are on that path explains why your team either scales or stalls.

You'll see this CBA progression echoed throughout the book. It's the backbone of every transformation Alex and his team experience.

This is the Hero Trap diagnostic. If you recognize three or more signs, the trap is already closing.

Five Signs You're Stuck in the Hero Trap

This is the entry diagnostic—not a measurement of where you are on the journey, but a recognition test. If three or more signs land, the trap is already closing. You don't need to score yourself yet. You need to see yourself.

- **Calendar test:** More than twenty meetings in a workweek where you're the decider; vacations require prework because things stop without you.
- **Delegation disappointment:** You say, "It's faster if I do it"; projects stall without your direction.
- **Growth paradox:** More people, slower motion; you're working harder with diminishing returns.
- **Development stagnation:** Team executes but doesn't develop judgment; succession feels impossible.
- **Stress signal:** You feel indispensable and overwhelmed; proud of being the go-to, exhausted by the responsibility.

For the complete HERO-to-ARCH Diagnostic, see appendix I (access the appendices at catalystgrowthadvisors.com/the-hero-trap/*).*

These patterns feel like strength. They're early warning signs . . .

These aren't five problems. They're five symptoms of one design: an organization that can't function without you.

You can't escape what you can't see.

But even when you see it, the pattern doesn't feel like a problem. It feels like caring.

Most leaders don't set out to create stress at work.

They care about their people. They want strong results. When things get unclear or start to slip, they step in to help. That instinct is understandable and is often rewarded early in a career.

The problem is what happens next.

When people don't have clear priorities, clear roles, or clear decision rights, their nervous systems treat that ambiguity as a threat. Stress increases. Attention narrows. People become more cautious and less cognitively flexible. This isn't a mindset issue. It's biology. Research in stress neuroscience shows that uncertainty reliably activates threat responses that impair the brain's executive functions, especially under sustained pressure.[4]

From a human standpoint, chronic uncertainty takes a toll. Repeated stress accumulates in the body over time, affecting energy, resilience, and long-term health. Leaders who care about their teams should understand this plainly: Clarity isn't just nice. It's protective.

From a performance standpoint, the effects are just as real. Under stress, the brain deprioritizes planning, judgment, and creative problem-solving. The very capabilities modern organizations depend on as complexity grows. You don't get people's best thinking when they're busy scanning for risk.

This creates a familiar pattern.

As uncertainty rises, leaders compensate by doing more. They make the decisions. They clarify things informally. They become the source of stability. In the short term, it works. In the long term, it makes the system dependent on them and keeps everyone else in a low-grade state of uncertainty.

That's the Hero Trap.

This book is about how capable, well-intentioned leaders fall into this pattern and how to build teams that are calm, clear, and effective without requiring constant heroic effort.

But first, it helps to understand why the trap is so easy to fall into and so hard to see from the inside.

Why Leaders Make the Same Predictable Mistake

Alex's trap isn't unique to him or even to start-up CEOs. It's the predictable result of a fundamental mismatch that catches every successful leader who transitions from individual contributor to organizational leader.

The problem isn't that heroes are bad leaders. It's that hero strategies that work brilliantly at a small scale become organizational constraints at a larger scale. But most leaders don't realize they're using the wrong strategy because the feedback loop is delayed.

When you're a Controller solving problems directly:

- **Immediate feedback:** Problem solved, crisis averted, results achieved
- **Delayed consequence:** Team learns to depend on you rather than develop capability

When you're an Architect building systems:

- **Immediate cost:** Slower progress, more meetings, teaching time
- **Delayed benefit:** Team becomes more capable, decisions improve, scaling accelerates

The Controller approach feels more productive because you get immediate positive feedback. The Architect approach feels slower because the benefits compound over months, not days.

The pressure to act fast is rarely about the situation. It's usually about your discomfort with not knowing.

This is why willpower alone never works for leadership transformation. Your brain is getting rewarded for the very behaviors that limit your organization's growth.

The Hero's Dilemma

Heroes approach the followership challenge through personal dominance. They try to become so impressive—so charismatic, visionary, or competent—that people follow them despite their natural wariness. The hero's implicit theory is that sufficiently powerful individual traits can override evolutionary psychology.

This creates a specific version of the hero's dilemma: the Hero Trap. The very traits that make someone seem leadership-worthy (confidence, decisiveness, ambition) are often the same traits that activate people's oppression detectors. The more heroic the leader acts, the more follower resistance they generate.

At ParagonCX, Alex Chen found himself in this situation. When a major customer threatened to churn, he stepped in with bold confidence, reassuring the client directly, dictating pricing changes, and directing product fixes overnight. The team rallied behind him during the crisis. But once the account was secure, the glow faded. Engineers asked why they had to wait for Alex's word before fixing obvious issues. Sales leaders wondered why they couldn't run pricing experiments themselves. What looked like strength in the moment revealed a deeper weakness: The team had learned to wait for Alex, not to act without him.

This is the Hero Trap in action: Traits that inspire in a crisis often backfire once stability returns. It explains why so many promising leaders burn out, why teams perform well under crisis but struggle during normal operations, and why employee engagement scores remain stubbornly low despite massive investments in leadership development.

This is the difference between heroic and architectural thinking. Heroes try to become so personally compelling that people follow despite their natural wariness. Architects design conditions that make following feel natural because it genuinely serves followers' interests.

Breaking Free: Design Culture That Reinforces Architect Identity

The hero identity served you well when problems were simpler and organizations were smaller. Now it constrains what your organization can achieve. But the solution isn't eliminating your expertise. It's systematically designing a culture that makes Architect behavior feel more natural than hero behavior.

Steering harder won't stop a car from drifting on ice. The more you fight it, the worse it gets.

> **Most leaders try to change through willpower. Architect leaders change through system design.**

The shift: Just like you can't run your way out of quicksand, you can't outwork a system designed to depend on you. But you can redesign it.

The hero habit got you here. The Architect's lens will propel you beyond it. From here on, your value won't come from fixing what's broken but from designing what stays whole.

Stop trying to be more worthy of following. Start building systems that make following feel like the smart choice.

IDENTITY = DESIGN (WHO YOU CHOOSE TO BE)

- Identity is intentional and declared.
- It's your designed leadership narrative: "I build systems and develop capability."

- You actively choose and articulate it.
- It answers: "Who am I as a leader? What makes me different from a hero leader?"

CULTURE = DEFAULT (HOW YOU ACTUALLY BEHAVE)

- Culture is often unconscious and emergent.
- It's your default behavior system—the habits, reflexes, and patterns that show up without design.
- It answers: "How do I lead when financial pressure hits? What do I default to in crisis?"

Your Leadership Opportunity

You can't just declare Architect identity and assume your behavior will follow. You must architect systems—decision rights, information flows, recognition patterns, meeting structures, escalation pathways—so that your default behaviors reinforce your designed identity.

In other words:

- Architect identity without supporting systems is empty words.
- Hero culture without identity clarity creates drift.

> **Design beats default when you close the gap between who you say you are and how you actually behave under financial pressure.**

This book will show you how to make that systematic transformation, step by step, from heroic leadership patterns to architectural thinking through deliberate culture design.

But first, you need to understand something that even most leadership experts miss: The real reason people follow isn't what you think it is. And until you understand the true psychology of followership, every attempt at transformation will fail.

Where the Real Shift Begins

Alex closed his laptop and exhaled. The patterns he was seeing weren't just operational failures. They were reflections of him. Every system he'd built still ran through his instincts, his judgment, his presence.

Alex wasn't losing control. He was losing his identity. And until he confronted that truth, nothing in his company would change.

The Signal Box

The same instincts that built your reputation are now binding your organization's capacity.

Key insights from this chapter:

- Heroes scale themselves; Architects scale the system.
- The Hero Trap closes through success, not failure—every problem you solve personally is a problem your organization never learns to solve.
- Controller feedback is immediate (problem solved); Architect feedback is delayed (capability built)—which is why willpower alone never works.
- The five signs of the trap aren't five problems—they're five symptoms of one design: an organization that can't function without you.
- Identity is what you declare; culture is what you default to. Design closes the gap.

When your organization's design no longer revolves around your presence, you've started the shift from Controller to Architect.

> **If you remember only one thing: The organization shaped itself around your brilliance. Now your brilliance is the constraint.**

Learning Prompt

Think about your own leadership challenge using the three-identity framework.

First, identify your current followership identity patterns. In which situations do you operate as Controller, Builder, or Architect?

Next, consider your most engaged team member and your least engaged team member. What's different about how they relate to the work, the team, and the mission? How might your leadership identity be contributing to these different levels of engagement?

Finally, choose one relationship in which you want to evolve from Controller to Builder or from Builder to Architect. What would change if you focused on designing systems that generate confidence rather than trying to be personally more confident?

CHAPTER 2

Stop Solving, Start Seeing

Thinking in Systems, Not Symptoms

Solving the same problem brilliantly twice isn't excellence. It's systems failure.

The night hadn't ended when the laptop closed. Alex's body was still in the kitchen, but his mind was back in every meeting, rearguing every decision. Even when the room was dark, the Slack pings echoed in his head. Sleep had become a form of deferred maintenance—something he'd fix when the fires stopped. But they never stopped.

Alex stared at the kitchen window for another ten minutes after closing his laptop. The house was quiet, but his mind raced through the same loop: customer escalation, broken road map, team dependencies, investor pressure. Every problem felt urgent. Every solution created three new problems.

He'd been the smartest person in the room for so long that he'd forgotten how to build rooms full of people smarter than he was.

The next morning, Alex walked into the office with a single question: What if the problem wasn't that he needed to work harder, but that he needed to think differently about problems entirely?

But first, he had to understand why some leaders could manage unimaginable complexity while he was drowning in just a fraction of it.

A system is a collection of interrelated parts that work together toward a common purpose.

—RUSSELL ACKOFF

Hero leadership is about fixing what's in front of you. Systems thinking is about seeing the whole—the forest, not just the trees. A single tree can only grow so tall, but a forest creates capabilities no tree can achieve alone.

When Andy Jassy became CEO of Amazon in 2021, he inherited what many called unmanageable complexity: retail, cloud computing, advertising, logistics, entertainment, and artificial intelligence—each business large enough to be a Fortune 500 company.

Most leaders would have simplified by divesting businesses or centralizing control. Jassy did the opposite. He doubled down on "organizational systems that enable complexity rather than constrain it."

The insight driving his approach was simple. Amazon's advantage did not live inside any single business. It lived in the interconnected systems that allowed those businesses to strengthen one another. Within eighteen months under Jassy's systems approach, Amazon achieved measurable results: strong growth in AWS despite intense competition, record logistics efficiency, breakthrough AI capabilities that leveraged data across units, and higher employee satisfaction as coordination became easier, not harder. The key was not heroic leadership. It was architectural thinking that designed systems to handle complexity automatically.

Not all systems do this well.

At ParagonCX, Alex tried to "add process" by requiring his approval on every cross-team change. Escalations dropped for a week—and then exploded. Work stalled because the new "system" was just Alex by another name. It taught the team to route more decisions to him, not fewer.

The Same Prevention Logic

In 2014, CVS applied the same logic Amazon had used when CVS stopped selling tobacco, giving up $2 billion in annual revenue. While competitors worked downstream—managing the consequences of tobacco-related diseases through better treatments—CVS went upstream to prevent those illnesses from occurring at all. It was the same shift Expedia made when it discovered that 58 percent of customers called for help after booking—and instead of hiring more support agents, it eliminated the confusion that caused the calls.[1] In both cases, the shift became obvious once they asked the right question: What if we prevented the problem instead of just managing it better?

That upstream principle also underpinned W. Edwards Deming's approach to quality. See the box to learn more about Deming's philosophy and how you can apply it in your own work.

QUALITY SCIENCE BOX
Deming's Prevention Framework

W. Edwards Deming transformed quality thinking by distinguishing between two types of problems:[2]

- **special causes addressed through direct problem-solving (roughly 5–20 percent)**
    - unique incidents requiring individual intervention
    - unpredictable events outside normal system variation
- **common causes addressed through system redesign (roughly 80–95 percent)**
    - predictable issues built into the system itself
    - recurring patterns indicating design flaws

The exact ratio varies, but the principle holds: Most problems are systemic, not personal.

WHAT THIS MEANS FOR YOUR CALENDAR

Think about last week. How many hours did you spend in meetings, on calls, or solving problems? For most leaders, it's twenty-five to thirty-five hours—more than half the week.

Now ask yourself: How many of those problems were truly unique, and how many were recurring in slightly different forms? Even using a conservative 80/20 split, that means three to four full days each week are spent solving the same types of problems again and again.

That's the Hero Trap: reacting faster without changing the system.

If 80–95 percent of your problems are baked into the system, no amount of personal responsiveness will buy you back your week. Only redesign reduces the volume. That's why Architects work upstream. It's the only place the math changes.

THE ARCHITECT'S REVERSAL

Architects work in the opposite direction. They dedicate a few hours each week to preventing one type of recurring problem from happening again. Over time, each fix frees capacity permanently—first for themselves, then for their teams.

Now imagine this shift cascading through your organization:

- You spend 25 hours a week on problem-solving.
- Your five direct reports each spend the same 25 hours (125 hours total).
- Their twenty-five team leads spend 25 hours each (625 hours total).

That's 775 hours per week consumed by problem-solving across the organization.

If even 80 percent of that time is spent on recurring issues, that's 620 hours per week—the equivalent of fifteen full-time salaries (based on a 40-hour workweek)—devoted to solving the same problems in new disguises. And the higher you go, the more expensive the distraction—not just in salary, but in growth that never happens.

When you and your leaders adopt the Architect mindset, those hours don't just get recovered—they get repurposed. The time you once spent fighting fires becomes time spent designing better systems, developing people, and moving strategy forward.

Architects don't just save time and money; they create time and momentum. The organization becomes faster, clearer, and more capable—not because people are working harder, but because the system itself is doing more of the work.

Deming's deeper insight wasn't just about quality—it was about how leaders allocate their most finite resource: attention. Controllers spend it solving today's problems. Architects invest it preventing tomorrow's.

This prevention mindset is just the beginning. But once leaders make the shift from solving to preventing, a new challenge emerges: designing systems that hold under pressure.

Many organizations have systems that work under normal conditions yet break when the pressure rises. What Amazon built were stable systems that produce predictable outcomes even when conditions change. Stable systems self-correct when they drift, get stronger under pressure instead of breaking down, and work whether you are there or not.

Appendix II ("Architect Systems in Practice") shows how Toyota achieved this kind of stability (access the appendices at *catalystgrowthadvisors.com/the-hero-trap/*). Through *jidoka*—the principle of built-in quality—and the *andon cord*, Toyota created a system that surfaces variation immediately, corrects it in real time, and strengthens the whole process under pressure. Toyota's results show that reliability isn't the product of discipline alone, but of design.

In a complex world, chaotic systems are often worse than no systems at all. There is a reason leaders resist this shift. Your brain fights it. To understand why, you have to look at how the mind processes complexity and why it defaults to heroic solutions even when systems would work better.[3]

Strategy Requires Systems Thinking

Heroes often excel at strategic thinking, but usually only half of it. They read markets, competitors, and customers. They spot opportunities and make bold external moves that create immediate advantage.

What they miss is the other half of strategy, the internal architecture that sustains advantage over time.

Traditional strategy focused on external positioning, where to compete, how to differentiate, which customers to serve. That maps to the hero's strength: individual impact on market outcomes. Heroes love conversations about market share and threats because those feel solvable through direct action.

Strategy today is broader. It is a lasting way to create and capture value, built on what we offer and how we operate, through a system of interdependent activities and capabilities.

At ParagonCX, Alex could describe the market play in detail, but the handoffs between sales, product, and success weren't designed. Opportunities were won in the field and then lost in the operating model. Once the team mapped the handoffs and set simple decision rules for each step, cycle time fell and fewer deals slipped through the cracks—not because anyone worked harder, but because the system stopped leaking.

What Alex experienced was a microcosm of a larger truth: When leaders rely on hero moves without designing the underlying architecture, strategy can't sustain itself.

The limits of hero strategy show up fast:

- Heroes optimize for external wins without building internal systems. Opportunities are captured, then eroded.
- Heroes create strategy dependencies. When the hero isn't available to coordinate, strategic momentum stalls.
- Heroes build strategy around personal capacity rather than organizational capability.

When the external environment shifts faster than the hero can respond, the competitive advantage becomes a liability.

Remember the invisible explosion from the introduction—twelve systems, eight teams, forty-seven handoff points triggered by a single customer complaint? That complexity didn't emerge because anyone designed it. It accumulated while everyone was solving problems.

This is where systems thinking becomes essential. Not as an intellectual framework, but as survival equipment.

BEHAVIORAL SCIENCE BOX
Why Your Brain Prefers Heroics Over Systems

Daniel Kahneman's research reveals why leaders default to heroic problem-solving even when systematic approaches would work better:

- **The *availability heuristic*** makes recent, memorable events seem more likely than they actually are. When you solve a problem directly, you create vivid memories of control and impact. When systems prevent problems, there's no memorable moment—just the absence of drama.
- **The *control illusion*** makes people overestimate their ability to influence outcomes through personal involvement. Directly solving problems creates the feeling of control, even when it's less effective than systematic prevention.
- **The *dopamine response*** creates an addiction to immediate problem-solving. Your brain releases dopamine when you successfully resolve urgent situations. This neurochemical reward makes firefighting feel more satisfying than fire prevention, even when prevention is objectively superior. Your brain literally becomes addicted to firefighting.

The neurological insight: Your brain is wired to prefer symptom-solving, but sustainable leadership requires consciously developing prevention reflexes.

Every cognitive bias in this box pulls you toward heroics. Every system you build pulls you toward freedom.

Why Systems Thinking Matters: From Looking Down to Looking Out

Controllers look *down* at problems requiring their intervention. Builders look *across* at patterns requiring capability development. Architects look *out* at system design opportunities that prevent problems entirely.

Traditional leaders look down at complexity and try to control it through personal involvement. The more time spent looking down, the less time remains to look out at opportunity.

> **This is the shift from "hands on everything" to "eyes on, hands off."**

Controllers keep hands on operational execution—personally involved in decisions, coordination, and problem-solving. Their attention stays consumed by what needs their direct involvement.

Architects maintain eyes on mission and outcomes while keeping hands off the execution. They monitor system health, not individual tasks. This frees their strategic attention to look out at opportunities rather than down at operations.

The goal isn't detachment—it's designing systems that enable visibility without requiring constant personal intervention.

Systems thinking flips that equation. Design systems that handle complexity automatically so you can look out at market shifts, emerging opportunities, and future moves. This is not only about efficiency. It is about reclaiming your strategic brain.

Chicago's approach to homelessness perfectly illustrates this shift from looking down to looking out. Like many major cities, Chicago had been struggling with growing homelessness for years. City leaders looked down at the operational complexity of shelter management—bed capacity, staffing, services, crisis response. They became expert coordinators, managing the downstream consequences of homelessness with impressive efficiency.

But when they finally looked out at the broader system, they discovered something surprising: Many people became homeless not because of complex social issues, but because they couldn't absorb small financial setbacks—a car repair, medical bill, or temporary job loss. The upstream solution was almost embarrassingly simple: Provide small emergency payments to prevent homelessness rather than manage it after it occurs.[4]

The leaders who had been consumed by shelter operations suddenly had the strategic capacity to address root causes. One system fix prevented thousands of individual crises.

The same pattern plays out when operational complexity exceeds heroic capacity, whether in city services or airline operations.

JetBlue's Valentine's Day Reckoning

February 14, 2007. JetBlue Airways passengers sat trapped on planes for up to eleven hours at New York's JFK Airport during an ice storm. No food service after the first few hours. Overflowing lavatories. Crying children. Furious business travelers missing critical meetings. And a leadership team that discovered—too late—that heroic effort couldn't overcome the absence of systems.

CEO David Neeleman personally called hundreds of passengers to apologize. Gate agents worked eighteen-hour shifts trying to coordinate rebookings manually. Operations managers made thousands of individual judgment calls about which planes to deice first, which crews to deploy where, which passengers to prioritize. Everyone was working heroically.

The heroics failed anyway. Over one thousand flights were canceled. The airline's reputation suffered damage that took years to repair. The problem wasn't a lack of effort or commitment—it was that JetBlue had built its rapid growth on individual excellence rather than systematic intelligence.

Looking Down

JetBlue's leaders had been focused on the daily heroics that enabled their customer service reputation—friendly crew members, flexible policies, personal touches that competitors had automated away. They looked down at each customer interaction, each operational challenge, each day's execution.

The Crisis Revealed What They Weren't Looking At

Weather prediction integration with crew scheduling. Automated passenger communication systems. Deicing protocol prioritization frameworks. Backup decision-making architecture that didn't require executives to coordinate every choice. System capacity for handling cascading disruptions. The crisis forced them to look out at what they'd been missing: the architectural systems that would prevent heroics from being necessary in the first place.

Great leaders flex between Controller, Builder, and Architect as conditions change. Their compass remains fixed on creating systems that outlast them.

The Systems They Built

Within six months, JetBlue had implemented the Customer Bill of Rights (the first in the industry), systematic weather response protocols, crew scheduling redundancy, and passenger communication automation. They didn't just apologize for the Valentine's Day disaster. They redesigned their operating architecture so that weather disruptions would never again require heroic leadership to manage.

The result wasn't just better crisis management. It was strategic capacity. Leaders who had been consumed by operational firefighting could now focus on competitive strategy, market expansion, and service innovation. One architectural transformation prevented thousands of individual crises.

What JetBlue faced at scale, every leader faces in miniature—the moment when heroic effort reaches its limit and the absence of systems becomes visible.

From Crisis to Recognition

Chicago's homelessness intervention. JetBlue's operational redesign. Different domains, same insight: Heroic individual effort has a ceiling, but systematic intelligence scales.

Alex Chen was about to discover this pattern in his own company—though his crisis would involve engineering backlogs and sales promises rather than weather delays and stranded passengers.

ParagonCX Discovers the Forest

Three months after that sleepless night when everything became clear, Alex Chen faced a new wave of problems at ParagonCX. As the head count rose from thirty-five to fifty, issues multiplied faster than he could solve them. Sales promised features not on the road map. Customer success needed data that engineering said would take months. Marketing drove leads that sales could not convert. Engineering built features that customers did not use.

Alex jumped in everywhere. He brokered meetings, wrote requirements, and approved messaging. The harder he worked, the worse it got.

"Alex, we do not have five separate problems," Maya said. "We have one system problem showing up in five places."

At the whiteboard, Alex drew connections: sales promises, road map conflicts, unused features, missing data, unconvertible leads. The picture emerged. The root was information flow. Nobody knew what anybody else was doing.

"What if," Alex asked, "instead of me being the hub, we designed systems where the right information flows to the right people automatically?"

That was the turning point. He stopped solving the leaves and started tending the root.

The Math Behind the Insight

This wasn't just Alex having an insight. It was the systems complexity explosion in action. With fifty people and 1,225 potential relationships, individual coordination becomes impossible. Ten-minute weekly check-ins with your forty-nine colleagues would consume eight hours—20 percent of your workweek—just to stay roughly aligned.

Alex had been manufacturing complexity for three years—every system added, every heroic save made, every exception approved—without seeing the accumulated weight. Now the math showed him what his exhaustion had been trying to tell him: The gap between what he could hold in his head and what he was accountable for had been widening every quarter. He just hadn't had a name for it until now.

Systems complexity requires systems thinking. This isn't philosophical—it's mathematically necessary when connections grow exponentially faster than human cognitive capacity.

When leaders make this shift, something else happens: Intelligence itself changes scale. No longer is the organization dependent on the smartest person in the room. Well-designed systems allow knowledge to circulate, perspectives to connect, and better answers to emerge. Collective intelligence is not about adding more brains—it's about designing conditions where the whole learns faster and solves problems better than any individual ever could.

That moment at the whiteboard completed a journey that had started months earlier when he was drowning in his kitchen at 3:17 a.m. The transition from hero to Architect wasn't an instant revelation—it was a series of insights that built on each other.

This insight marked Alex's first real transition from Controller thinking to Architect design. Instead of being the solution or teaching others to be solutions, he began designing systems that created solutions.

Alex's systems breakthrough felt like a victory. He had no idea that getting people to use those systems would be an entirely different battle.

Reflection: Where am I unintentionally teaching my team that I must be the answer?

For systematic tools to apply these concepts, see appendix I: the Systems Building Canvas for designing prevention systems, the Complexity Debt Audit for surfacing hidden dependencies, and the Wicked Problem Diagnostic Method for distinguishing systemic causes from human ones (access the appendices at catalystgrowthadvisors.com/the-hero-trap/*).*

The Signal Box

Heroes treat symptoms one at a time; Architects redesign the system that keeps producing them.

Key insights from this chapter:

- Recurring problems aren't asking for better solutions—they're asking for systems.
- Looking down solves today's problem; looking out reveals the design that prevents tomorrow's.
- Systems complexity grows exponentially while individual capacity grows linearly—a fifty-person team has 1,225 possible relationships.
- One architectural fix prevents thousands of individual crises (Chicago's homelessness intervention, JetBlue's Customer Bill of Rights).
- The shift from Controller to Architect begins when you stop tending leaves and start tending the root.

When you find yourself solving the same problem for the third time, the problem isn't the problem—the design is.

> **If you remember only one thing: Recurring problems aren't asking for better solutions—they're asking for systems.**

Learning Prompt

Here's what I've noticed: Some decisions I make repeatedly seem to get better over time, while others stay just as difficult no matter how many times I face them.

Think about that recurring decision you identified. Has it gotten easier to make well over time, or does it still require the same mental energy each time?

If it hasn't gotten easier, that might be a signal that it needs a system rather than more experience. What would need to be true for someone else to make this decision as well as you do?

The test: Design it and see whether the system makes the decision easier or better. Sometimes our theories about what works get challenged by reality.

CHAPTER 3

Why They Follow You (and Why That's the Problem)

The leaders everyone follows are often the ones no one should follow.

Two months after Alex Chen's systems thinking breakthrough at ParagonCX, he was about to discover an uncomfortable truth about transformation: Identity evolution isn't linear across all domains.

For the first time in years, Alex had felt like he was ahead of the problems instead of buried under them. The meetings ran smoother, the fires stayed small, and people stopped coming to him for every decision.

But the quiet didn't feel like peace. It felt like distance. The energy that used to pulse through late-night Slack threads had been replaced by polite efficiency. People were following the system perfectly—and somehow, that made it worse. The organization was humming, but he couldn't feel its heartbeat.

While Alex had begun developing Architect capabilities for problem-solving and process design, his approach to team relationships remained trapped in Controller patterns. The frameworks and systems he'd built were working, but his leadership identity was about to be tested in a completely different arena.

The technical problems that used to explode into crises were now being prevented systematically. Customer escalations that once required Alex's personal intervention were now being handled by the team. Revenue targets were being hit.

But the voluntary turnover hadn't slowed. If anything, it was accelerating.

This time, it was Jessica, a senior product manager who'd been with ParagonCX for three years. She asked for time to talk, and Alex already knew what was coming.

"I'm not leaving because the work isn't interesting," she said, choosing her words carefully. "And I'm not leaving because of the mission. I believe in what we're building."

Alex waited, his face betraying his feelings.

"It's just . . . the systems you've created are really good. The processes work. But they're all designed to execute your vision, make your decisions easier to scale, reflect your priorities." She paused. "I don't feel like I'm building something. I feel like I'm operating machinery that someone else designed."

Alex felt the familiar sting of contradiction. He'd spent two months building systems specifically to reduce dependency on him. "But you have more autonomy now than ever," he said. "You don't have to check with me on every decision anymore."

"That's true," Jessica acknowledged. "But I'm not making decisions—I'm following the decision framework you built. I'm not setting priorities—I'm implementing the prioritization system you designed. The systems work without you being in the room. But they still come from you."

After she left, Alex sat in the conference room staring at the whiteboard covered with his system diagrams. Every process, every framework, every documented workflow—all of it reflected his thinking, his priorities, his approach to problem-solving.

He'd built better systems. He hadn't changed a damn thing about himself.

The answer lay in a fundamental truth about leadership transformation: Building better systems while maintaining Controller relationship patterns creates a more sophisticated form of dependency, not independence.

The Followership Fallacy

Alex had fallen victim to what I call the followership fallacy—the mistaken belief that great leaders naturally create great followers. It's the assumption that if you build better systems, make smarter decisions, and solve problems more effectively, people will naturally want to follow your lead.

But here's what Alex didn't understand: The very behaviors that made him successful as an individual contributor were systematically destroying his team's willingness to think independently. Every problem he solved personally was a problem his organization never learned to solve systematically. And now, every system he built personally was a system his organization never learned to build collaboratively.

He'd learned about systems thinking and built frameworks to prevent recurring problems. Progress—except he'd done it alone. The systems worked, but they were *his* systems. People still felt like followers—just followers of well-designed processes instead of chaotic heroics.

The Leadership Multiplication Effect

The ten submarine captains who emerged from Captain Marquet's *Santa Fe* represented something unprecedented in naval leadership: a systematic approach to developing leaders who could succeed anywhere. This wasn't about creating loyal followers who would stay forever—it was about building capability that strengthened the entire submarine force.[1]

Richard Branson captured this paradox perfectly: "Train people well enough so they can leave, treat them well enough so they don't want to." The architectural insight lies in understanding both parts working together.

The first part—training people so well they could leave—isn't about retention at all. It's about building such deep capability throughout your organization that any departure becomes an opportunity for someone else to step up, rather than a crisis that threatens everything.

The second part—treating them well enough so they don't want to leave—becomes possible only when you're not desperately clinging to any individual. When you know that great people leaving is OK because you've systematically developed others who can grow into those opportunities, you can focus on creating an environment so compelling that most choose to build their careers with you.

The Harder Puzzle

In chapter 1, we asked why anyone would willingly surrender autonomy to follow another person's vision. Alex was now facing a harder version of that puzzle: Why do people still feel like followers even when you've built systems to prevent that?

Jessica hadn't left because Alex was making all the decisions. She left because the systems made all the decisions—Alex's systems, reflecting Alex's priorities, executing Alex's vision. The dependency hadn't disappeared. It had just become more sophisticated.

People don't just resist heroic leaders. They resist any leadership approach that makes them feel like operators rather than Builders, followers rather than members.

Our evolutionary history makes this even more striking. Muzafer Sherif's famous Robbers Cave experiment demonstrates this perfectly. In 1954, Sherif brought twenty-two eleven-year-old boys to a summer camp and separated them into two groups. Initially, both groups were egalitarian and cooperative, making decisions collectively with little interest in formal hierarchy.

Then Sherif introduced competition between the groups. The transformation was immediate. Boys who had been collaborative decision-makers suddenly looked to the most assertive members for leadership. The moment external competition appeared, our evolved capacity for hierarchical coordination was activated.[2]

So humans have a dual nature: We're simultaneously anti-authoritarian and capable of hierarchical coordination (what Jonathan Haidt calls our "chimp/bee" nature[3]). This creates a design challenge for anyone trying to lead: How do you activate people's capacity for followership without triggering their oppression detectors?

The Three Leadership Identities and Followership

Different leadership identities create fundamentally different follower experiences—and trigger different psychological responses.

- **Controller followership ("Follow me"):** Controllers create confidence through personal competence and direct involvement. This feels dependent to followers: "I need the leader to succeed" and "I wait for direction before acting."
- **Builder followership ("Follow this approach"):** Builders create confidence through systematic capability development and proven frameworks. This feels developmental: "I'm growing my capabilities" and "I use proven approaches."
- **Architect followership ("Follow this purpose"):** Architects create confidence through system reliability and collective intelligence. This feels independent: "I make good decisions using our systems" and "This works whether I'm here or not."

Followers need you. Members need the mission. The shift from Controller to Architect is the shift from one to the other.

The Followership Barter

Followership is fundamentally transactional: People entrust part of their future to a leader only when they get something in return. That "something in return" is confidence.

This reframes the entire leadership challenge. People don't follow because leaders are impressive—they follow because leaders create confidence in an uncertain future. The question shifts from "How do I become worth following?" to "How do I design systems that generate confidence?"

Alex's systems had failed this test. They were efficient, but they didn't generate confidence—they generated compliance. Jessica's exit proved it.

Captain Marquet discovered this on the USS *Santa Fe*. Instead of perfecting command and control, he systematically gave control to his crew, developing leaders at every level.

The *Santa Fe* went from worst to first in the entire fleet. The "leader-leader" model became standard training across the submarine force—proof that architectural leadership consistently produces better results than traditional heroic leadership.

The Breakthrough Understanding

The most sophisticated research on transformational leadership reveals something remarkable: Effective leaders don't create followers at all. They create *members*.

- **Followers depend on the leader:** They need constant direction, motivation, and decision-making from above.
- **Members are interdependent within a system:** They coordinate naturally because they share identity, purpose, and mutual accountability.

The difference is profound and measurable:

- **Followers ask:** "What does the leader want me to do?"
- **Members ask:** "What does our mission need from me?"

- **Followers think:** "I work for this person."
- **Members think:** "We work toward this purpose."

- **Followers worry:** "Will the leader approve of my work?"
- **Members worry:** "Will this serve our collective success?"

- **Followers depend:** On constant direction and feedback.
- **Members coordinate:** Through shared standards and mutual accountability.

Robert Hogan and Robert Kaiser's research summary captures this beautifully: "Transformational leadership changes the way followers see themselves—from isolated individuals to members of a larger group. Transformational leaders do this by modeling collective commitment (through self-sacrifice and the use of 'we' rather than 'I'), emphasizing the similarity of group members, and reinforcing collective goals, shared values, and common interests."[4]

Marcus Buckingham's research highlights a crucial tension: People want to feel part of something larger than themselves while also being valued as unique individuals. At first glance, these needs seem contradictory, but together they define the essence of architectural leadership—designing systems that cultivate shared purpose without erasing individuality.[5]

You can see this transformation in how Captain Marquet's crew described their work on the USS *Santa Fe*. Before the change, sailors would say things like "Request permission to submerge." After the shift to intent-based leadership, they said instead "I intend to submerge the ship." The language signaled a deeper identity change—from actions attributed to the captain to ownership claimed by the crew.[6]

The membership test: Walk through your workplace and listen to how people talk about their work. Do they say "My boss wants . . ." or "Our team needs . . ."? Do they refer to company goals as "their targets" or "our mission"? The language reveals whether you've created followers or members.

The Signal Box

Better systems without changed identity creates more sophisticated dependency, not independence.

Key insights from this chapter:

- Heroes create followers; Architects create members.
- Followers ask "What does the leader want?"; members ask "What does our mission need?"
- Followership is transactional—people entrust their future to a leader only when they get confidence in return.
- Compliance and confidence look similar from a distance, but only one survives your absence.

- The language test reveals the truth: "Alex wants" signals followership; "we need" signals membership.
- When your team's language shifts from "the leader" to "our mission," you've stopped creating followers and started building members.

> **If you remember only one thing: They're not following you—they're following who they become around you.**

Learning Prompt

Something I find fascinating: We've all been part of teams where we felt like authentic members (not just followers) of something important. We've also experienced the opposite—feeling like we were just waiting for direction.

Think about your most engaged team member and your least engaged team member. Before analyzing their differences, reflect: What was different about your own experience when you felt like a genuine member versus when you felt like a follower?

Now look at those two team members: What conditions might be creating membership versus followership experiences? How might your leadership identity be either enabling or blocking the conditions that create willing engagement?

The insight: When you understand what membership feels like from the inside, you can design systems that create that experience rather than just measuring its absence.

CHAPTER 4

From Control to Connection

Designing for Ownership

Members solve problems hiding in plain sight.

After Jessica's exit, Alex Chen had reached his breaking point. He hadn't expected it to sting that much. Systems were working, growth was steady, crises were down—this was when people were supposed to *stay*.

Instead, one of his best people had basically said, "What you built is good. I just don't see *myself* in it."

On the drive home that night, Alex realized he wasn't losing talent to compensation or chaos anymore. He was losing them to invisibility. They could execute inside his design, but they couldn't *belong* inside it.

His phone buzzed in the cupholder. Emma.

"Hey—running about twenty minutes late. The Jessica conversation went long."

Silence on the other end. Then: "Alex. The recital started at 5:30."

He glanced at the dashboard clock. 6:47.

"I thought it was—" He stopped. He knew exactly when it was. He'd put it in his calendar three weeks ago, then scheduled over it when Marcus flagged the Hendricks contract as urgent. He'd meant to move the meeting. He'd meant to protect the time. He'd meant to be there.

"Is it over?"

"Twenty minutes ago."

Alex pulled into a gas station parking lot to collect himself.

"How was she?"

"She was wonderful. She looked for you in the audience three times. I counted." Emma's voice was flat—past anger, past disappointment, somewhere in the territory of resignation. "I told her you had an emergency at work."

"I'll make it up to her. I'll—"

"You'll what, Alex? Take her to dinner? Buy her something?" Emma exhaled. "She doesn't want things. She wanted you in a chair, watching her be brave in front of strangers. That was tonight. It's gone now."

After Emma hung up, Alex sat in the parking lot for a long time. A fluorescent light buzzed overhead. Somewhere inside the gas station, someone was buying lottery tickets.

Jessica's words echoed back: *I don't see myself in it.*

Sophie had looked for him three times.

He'd built systems so his team could execute without him. But he hadn't built a life that could include him. He'd optimized for being needed at work, and the cost was becoming absent everywhere else.

He thought about the Hendricks contract, the one that had felt so urgent. He couldn't even remember what the issue was now.

Alex had built a structure with no windows. People couldn't see themselves in the work.

And somewhere along the way, his daughter had stopped expecting to see him at all.

The exit interviews from his departing top performers—Jessica included—had made the problem devastatingly clear: People weren't leaving ParagonCX because of the mission or opportunity. They were leaving because they felt like followers rather than leaders, operators of machinery someone else had designed.

But understanding the problem and solving it were two different things. How do you transform a hero-dependent organization into one that creates willing members?

The Inspiration Trap

Alex did what leaders do when they don't know what else to try. He called an all-hands.

He spent the weekend crafting what he told himself was a vision speech. Monday morning, forty-three people packed into the conference room. Alex stood at the front and felt the familiar flutter in his chest. He knew this feeling. It was the feeling of being needed.

For twenty minutes, he was *on*. He told the story of their first customer. He painted a picture of where ParagonCX could be in five years. He named people individually, connecting their work to outcomes that mattered.

The room leaned in. Someone in the back wiped their eyes.

And somewhere in minute fourteen, a thought flickered through his mind: *You love this.* Not the mission. Not the team. *This*—the attention, the energy, forty-three people looking at him like he had answers.

He pushed the thought away and finished strong.

Two weeks later, the hum was gone.

Not dramatically, just the slow return of familiar patterns. The same questions routed to Alex. The same language: *What does Alex want us to prioritize?*

In the Tuesday leadership meeting, Maya presented a road map identical to the one from before the all-hands. Same bottlenecks. Same assumption that Alex would resolve the conflicts.

"I thought we talked about this," Alex said. "About ownership."

Maya looked at him. Not angry. Tired.

"We did talk about it. You gave a really good speech." She paused. "And then nothing changed. The approval chains are the same. The decision rights are the same." She glanced around the table. "We felt inspired for a few days. But inspiration doesn't change how the system actually works."

"This isn't the first time," David added quietly. "You've given this talk before."

Alex opened his mouth, then closed it.

The room waited. He felt the heavy silence.

You can't talk people into ownership.

He'd known it before he called the all-hands. He'd known it during the speech. He'd known it when he saw the person wiping their eyes and felt the rush of being the one who moved them.

Inspiration wasn't the problem. Inspiration was the trap.

He'd been trying to change what people believed. But beliefs weren't the problem. The system was the problem—the system that made waiting for Alex the rational choice.

What if he stopped trying to inspire different behavior and started designing conditions that made different behavior inevitable?

The breakthrough came when Alex realized he needed to stop thinking like a Controller and start thinking like an Architect. Trying to steer every wave is exhausting. Designing the tide is leadership.

Instead of asking "How do I become a better leader?" he began asking "How do I design systems that naturally create the experiences people need?"

The answer lay in what psychologist Jonathan Haidt calls the *moral foundations of human cooperation.* These are the deep psychological structures that determine whether people experience leadership as legitimate or oppressive. This is combined with Marcus Buckingham's research on what makes followership measurable. Drawing on Haidt's foundations, I've identified three that matter most for organizational membership design: authority (legitimate coordination, not arbitrary domination), liberty (autonomy within structure), and loyalty (chosen membership, not imposed compliance).[1]

The Architect's Blueprint

Alex's task wasn't to inspire better followers. It was to design conditions where membership emerged naturally. Where following the system felt like serving your own interests, not just the leader's.

Throughout this book, I use *membership* to describe a condition of psychological ownership, decision agency, and safety to act in service of a shared mission. *Followership* describes a system in which commitment flows primarily to a visionary individual, authority concentrates upward, and capable people look to the leader for direction rather than to the work itself.

When authority is transparent, autonomy is real, and loyalty is shared, information moves, perspectives connect, and decisions improve through contribution at every level. Researchers call this *collective intelligence*—a concept pioneered at MIT's Center for Collective Intelligence—and it emerges only when systems are designed to enable it.[2]

Three foundations make this possible:

- **Authority:** People need to see leadership as legitimate coordination, not arbitrary domination.
- **Liberty:** People need to feel autonomous within structure, not oppressed by it.
- **Loyalty:** People need to experience membership as valuable and chosen, not imposed.

Think of these as load-bearing walls. Get any one wrong, and the whole structure becomes unstable. Get all three right, and genuine membership emerges.

The leadership identity challenge: Controllers create dependency across all three foundations—demanding compliance, prescribing methods, requiring personal loyalty. Builders develop capability, but people still depend on the leader's frameworks. Architects design systems where authority feels legitimate, autonomy is real, and loyalty connects to something larger than any individual.

Before Alex could redesign the three foundations, he needed to see his current reality clearly.

Your Followership Reality Check

By now you understand the Controller → Builder → Architect progression. The question for this chapter is more specific: **Are you creating followers or members?**

Here's the diagnostic that cuts through self-deception:

1. **Listen to your team's language for one week:** Don't change anything—just notice:

Follower signals (dependency language):

- "Alex wants us to . . ."
- "I'm waiting for approval on . . ."
- "I need to check with [you] before . . ."
- "What should I do about . . . ?"
- "I wanted to run this by you . . ."

Member signals (ownership language):

- "We decided to . . ."
- "I handled that by . . ."
- "Here's what we're trying . . ."
- "I noticed X so I . . ."
- "Our approach is . . ."

2. **Count the ratio:** If it's 3:1 or higher (follower to member language), you're creating dependency even if your systems are sophisticated.
3. **Now test your own instincts:** The next time someone brings you a problem, notice your first internal response:
   - **Controller instinct:** Mental solutions forming, urgency to fix it, satisfaction at having the answer.
   - **Builder instinct:** Questions forming about their thinking, impulse to coach them through it.
   - **Architect instinct:** Curiosity about why this problem reached you at all, wondering what system gap allowed it.

The followership diagnostic isn't about good or bad—it's about awareness. Most leaders discover they're Controllers in high-stress situations, Builders when they have time to coach, and Architects only in domains they've systematically redesigned.

Your move: Pick *one* recurring situation this week where you default to Controller mode (personally solving problems). Instead of solving it, ask: "What would need to be different in our systems for this problem not to reach me next time?"

That question is the bridge from creating followers to building members.

> *For systematic membership design, see the Membership Design Canvas, Buckingham Followership Diagnostic, and Oppression Detector Audit in appendix I (access the appendices at* catalystgrowthadvisors.com/the-hero-trap/*). These tools give you the complete assessment and planning frameworks when you're ready for deeper work.*

Run this diagnostic weekly until the ratio flips. That's when you'll know when design beats default.

Alex ran this diagnostic and discovered a 3:1 ratio of follower to member language. His team's instincts defaulted to waiting for his approval.

The ratio told him *what* was broken. Not *where.*

To find the source, he audited ParagonCX across the three foundations—looking for gaps between what his systems promised and what people actually experienced.

What he discovered wasn't pretty.

Foundation 1: Authority Without Domination

What the audit revealed: Decision-making processes were opaque—people didn't understand how or why choices got made. Most strategic decisions waited for Alex's input, creating bottlenecks that frustrated everyone. Authority felt arbitrary rather than systematic.

What Alex tested: In a single meeting, instead of making the decision about resource allocation, he walked the team through his thinking: customer data showing enterprise demand, competitive landscape pressuring their positioning, financial models determining viability.

"Here's the information I'm looking at," he explained. "Here's how I weigh competing priorities. What am I missing?"

The room came alive. Engineering saw technical constraints Alex hadn't considered. Sales understood customer urgency differently than the data suggested. Customer success identified renewal risks that would affect timing.

The final decision was better than what Alex would have made alone—and everyone understood why it made sense.

What he systematized: Over the next month, Alex created decision guides for their three most common strategic choices: resource allocation, pricing decisions, and product road map prioritization. Each guide spelled out what information to gather, which stakeholders to consult, how to weigh competing factors, and when to escalate.

ALEX'S AUTHORITY REDESIGN

- **Transparent decision processes:** Strategic decisions were documented—what information mattered, what trade-offs were considered.
- **Clear escalation criteria:** Decisions that needed his input were defined, as opposed to those that could proceed autonomously.
- **Systematic context sharing:** Strategic information—customer insights and competitive intelligence—was made accessible to everyone.

How he knew it worked: Priya, an account manager, used the pricing decision guide to approve a nonstandard contract. She documented her reasoning, consulted with finance and product, and made the call. The decision was sound—and Alex learned about it after the contract was signed.

Within weeks, people stopped waiting for Alex to decide. They had what they needed to make aligned decisions themselves.

Foundation 2: Liberty Within Structure

What the audit revealed: People felt micromanaged rather than empowered. They had clear goals but little autonomy over how to achieve them. The structure meant to create clarity had inadvertently created constraint.

The issue isn't structure itself—it's when structure makes people powerless. Controllers create false trade-offs: "Follow my vision exactly, or leave." Architects create liberty *through* structure, defining boundaries inside which people have full freedom.

What Alex tested: With the engineering team, instead of prescribing development methodologies, he defined outcome requirements: Features must be tested, documented, and deployable within sprint timeframes. How they got there was their call.

The team chose pair programming and continuous integration—approaches Alex hadn't suggested. Quality improved. Velocity increased.

What he systematized:

ALEX'S LIBERTY REDESIGN

- **Outcome authority, method freedom:** Teams controlled how they achieved outcomes. Engineering chose their development approaches within clear delivery standards. Customer success had the freedom to choose engagement methods as long as retention goals were met.
- **Veto powers:** Anyone could halt a customer deployment or marketing campaign if quality or brand were at risk. People had genuine authority, not just accountability.
- **Choice architecture:** Even when processes were fixed, teams could choose formats, tools, and timing. Small choices preserved autonomy while maintaining coordination.

How he knew it worked: Amir, a junior engineer, halted a customer deployment because he spotted a security vulnerability no one else had caught. It sent a clear signal: Authority wasn't about seniority. It was about judgment and responsibility.

People started proposing solutions rather than waiting for permission.

Foundation 3: Loyalty Through Chosen Membership

What the audit revealed: People felt like employees, not members. They were committed to paychecks, not to ParagonCX's mission. Team identity was weak. People worked in silos rather than as part of something larger.

Controllers try to inspire loyalty through personal magnetism—creating systems that collapse when the hero leaves. Architects build loyalty to the mission, values, and identity of the group itself.

What Alex tested: At the next all-hands, instead of giving another vision speech, Alex tried something different. He asked three people from different teams to share a customer story—not a success story, but a moment when they'd personally seen their work matter to someone.

The engineering lead, Marco, described a call in which a frustrated customer became an advocate after a bug fix. A support rep talked about a thank-you email she'd kept for two years. A sales manager admitted losing a deal and then explained what the team learned from it.

Alex said almost nothing. The room connected around a shared purpose rather than around him.

What he systematized:

ALEX'S LOYALTY REDESIGN

- **Similarity architecture:** Cross-functional teams, learning lunches, and quarterly off-sites emphasized what people had in common rather than departmental differences.
- **Synchrony design:** Rhythms and rituals connected daily work to the mission—customer stories at all-hands, weekly updates linking tasks to company goals, monthly retrospectives reinforcing shared learning.
- **Healthy competition:** Teams measured themselves against external benchmarks, not each other—customer success versus industry standards, engineering versus best practices, sales versus market performance.

How he knew it worked: Six weeks later, Maya mentioned something in passing: "Have you noticed people say 'we' more?" Alex hadn't noticed. But when he listened, she was right. The language had shifted—not because he'd asked for it, but because the system made membership feel real.

Together, the three foundations transformed ParagonCX. Authority gave confidence in process. Liberty gave confidence in capability. Loyalty gave confidence in belonging.

You can't talk people into ownership. You have to design the conditions that make ownership feel natural.

Proof That It Worked

Six months later, Alex turned to the Buckingham Followership Diagnostic to measure whether his redesign had changed anything.

The initial scores had been sobering: 21.5/40. People weren't enthusiastic about the mission (2.8/5), didn't feel challenged to grow (2.6/5), and lacked confidence that their teammates had their backs (2.4/5).

Six months after the redesign: 34.3/40. Every single measure improved dramatically. Mission enthusiasm jumped from 2.8 to 4.2. Confidence in the company's future rose from 3.1 to 4.6.

But the deepest signal appeared in language. Before the redesign, people said:

- "Alex wants us to focus on customer retention this quarter."
- "I need to check with Alex before changing that process."

After the redesign:

- "We need to improve retention because our customers are telling us . . ."
- "Our team decided to revise that process based on what we learned."

The shift from "Alex wants" to "we need" revealed a profound identity change, from followers dependent on Alex to members collectively responsible for ParagonCX's mission.

Alex heard it first in a Thursday stand-up. Maya was explaining a process change to the team—not asking permission, not checking with him, just *explaining what they'd decided.*

He thought about the all-hands six months ago. The speech he'd spent a weekend writing. The dopamine hit of forty-three people leaning in. How good it had felt. How little it had changed.

He hadn't stopped inspiring people—but he'd stopped expecting inspiration to do the structural work. He'd redesigned decision rights.

Changed information flows. Rebuilt the approval chains that Maya had called out. Architecture made the inspiration stick.

And here was Maya, owning something she never would have touched before.

He remembered something from Daryl Bem's research that his executive coach had shared: Identity follows behavior. Act like an Architect, watch yourself doing it, and you start believing you are one. That is, when you change the environment and the actions, the beliefs follow.[3]

Alex had stopped trying to convince people to think like owners. He'd built a system where they *acted* like owners—and became them.

Within six months of the redesign, decision speed increased 40 percent, initiative taking doubled, cross-functional collaboration surged, and retention of high performers climbed to 95 percent.

The numbers told the story.

Alex no longer carried the company by force of will. ParagonCX itself had become the system that carried its mission forward.

"The ultimate test wasn't whether they missed me," Alex reflected, "but whether they proved they didn't need me to do excellent work."

The Membership Design Imperative

Alex's journey demonstrates that the transition from heroic to architectural leadership isn't just theoretical—it's practically achievable. But it requires a fundamental shift in how leaders think about their value.

Architects don't stop asking, "How do I become more effective?" They add a second question: "How do I design systems that create the experiences people need to feel ownership over obligation, whether I'm in the room or not?" They channel personal charisma into systematic design that generates genuine membership.

Alex's crisis became his breakthrough because he learned to see followership as a design challenge rather than a personality contest. The same frameworks that transformed ParagonCX can transform any organization where leaders are ready to shift from hero to Architect.

The Signal Box

You can't talk people into ownership—you have to design the conditions that make ownership feel natural.

Key insights from this chapter:

- Inspiration without design creates moments; design makes inspiration last.
- Three foundations create membership: authority (legitimate coordination), liberty (autonomy within structure), and loyalty (chosen belonging).
- Identity follows behavior—change the environment and the actions, and the beliefs will follow.
- Controllers create dependency across all three foundations; Architects design systems where each foundation reinforces the others.
- The shift from "Alex wants" to "we need" reveals when architecture, not charisma, is doing the work.

When authority feels legitimate, autonomy is real, and loyalty connects to something larger than any individual, membership emerges on its own.

> **If you remember only one thing: Inspiration without design creates moments. Design creates inspiration that lasts.**

Learning Prompt

Most leaders believe they're creating empowering experiences for their teams. But team members don't always experience it that way.

This week, take the eight-question Buckingham Followership Diagnostic in appendix I to see how your team experiences membership (access the appendices at *catalystgrowthadvisors.com/the-hero-trap/*). Notice where scores surprise you—especially gaps between individual contribution and collective membership.

Pick *one* foundation—authority, liberty, or loyalty—where scores are lowest. If all three score similarly low, consider starting with authority. When people understand how and why decisions get made, they're more likely to use autonomy well and connect to a shared purpose. But trust your context—if you sense a different starting point would create faster momentum, start there.

The learning: The gap between what you think you're creating and what people experience reveals your highest-leverage opportunity.

FAST TRACK

Three Moves to Break the Hero Habit

Important: Read chapters 1–4 to understand the Controller → Builder → Architect framework and the three invisible forces that make transformation so difficult.

Before we dive into the complete hero-to-Architect transformation, here's how to start building systems that work without you right away. These three moves deliver the majority of the value—even if you never read another page.

Quick Start Support Options

You can work through these moves using the following frameworks.

Your Current Reality Check (Two to Five Minutes)

Ask yourself:

- When problems arise, do people automatically bring them to you?
- Do you feel valuable when solving urgent issues personally?
- Are you busier now than six months ago despite team growth?
- Do problems you've solved before keep recurring?
- Would operations slow significantly if you were unavailable for a week?

If you answered "yes" to three or more, you're operating in hero mode—and this Fast Track will help you start shifting immediately.

If you answered "no" to most questions, you may have already built these capabilities, or this may be better suited for a colleague facing these challenges right now. Keep reading if you want the complete framework.

Why Controller Mode Feels Inescapable

Remember the three invisible forces from the introduction:

- **Success patterns** trained you to be the hero—now that expertise constrains your team.
- **BANI conditions** require adaptation faster than you can personally process.
- **Systems complexity** exceeds individual capacity (a fifty-person team has 1,225 possible relationships).

These forces explain why Controller mode—which worked when you had ten relationships and quarterly planning cycles—breaks when complexity explodes exponentially.

The solution isn't eliminating Controller. Crisis and technical expertise still require direct action. You're expanding your repertoire so you can choose Controller, Builder, or Architect strategically based on what each situation demands—not what feels familiar.

The Paradigm in Practice

Most leaders default to Controller mode, even when Builder or Architect would create better results. These three moves help you recognize when you're stuck in Controller out of habit and start building your Builder and Architect capabilities. Each will feel uncomfortable, which is the signal you're expanding your repertoire:

- **Move 1** prevents problems instead of solving them faster (feels slow, but compounds).
- **Move 2** builds systems that work without you (feels risky, but scales).

- **Move 3** develops others' thinking instead of supplying answers (feels inefficient, but multiplies).

The discomfort is temporary. The exponential results are permanent.

Move 1: The Ten-Minute Prevention Reflex (Controller → Builder)

Start today.

Instead of solving your next problem, prevent the problem category. When someone brings you an issue, ask, "Have we seen this before?" If *no* (appears to be first occurrence):

- Crisis or time sensitive? Solve it directly. Controller mode is appropriate for genuine one-offs or urgent situations.
- Have ten-plus minutes? Solve it while teaching your thinking process. This is Builder mode: "Let me walk you through how I'd approach this . . ."

Why teach on apparent one-offs: You're developing judgment, not just solving problems. And what looks unique today might reveal tomorrow's pattern.

If *yes* (this category has happened before):

Solve the immediate problem as you normally would, then ask, "What would prevent this category from happening again?" Identify one system change that could eliminate the pattern. Schedule thirty minutes this week to design that prevention.

Example: A team member asks about handling a difficult client. Instead of just giving advice, create a simple communication framework so anyone can succeed in future situations. Ask yourself, What's the category of problem here? (Client expectations? Communication breakdowns? Scope creep?)

Why this works: You're not doing more work—just adding ten minutes that compound over time. Each prevented category means fewer interruptions later. You shift from endlessly solving individual problems to systematically eliminating problem types.

Move 2: The Netflix Test (Builder → Architect)

Start this week.

Reed Hastings, Netflix's cofounder and CEO, takes six weeks of vacation every year. When he steps away, Netflix continues operating at full capacity. The company doesn't just survive his absence—it maintains performance because Netflix has systematically built systems that reduce dependency on any single leader. The "Netflix test" asks the same question: If you stepped away, what would break first? That's where you need to build systems that run without you.

Find one area where you're still the bottleneck and build a system that runs without you.

Run the Netflix test: Close your eyes and imagine getting a call that you need to be unreachable for six weeks starting tomorrow. Which area makes your chest tighten? That's where you're still the hero instead of the Architect. Notice the specific scenarios playing in your mind—those urgent emails you imagine piling up, the decisions you picture stalling, the problems you see spiraling without your intervention.

That physical reaction tells you exactly where to focus your systems-building energy.

Steps:

1. **Feel the dependency first:** Don't just analyze which areas need you—notice where your body responds with anxiety or resistance to the idea of stepping away.
2. **Document what you do:** When that issue arises, what specific knowledge, judgment, or authority do you bring that others lack?
3. **Create the missing bridge:** Design a simple system (decision guide, authority matrix, communication template) that gives others what they need to handle it autonomously.
4. **Test with low stakes:** Try it for a week in a situation where failure won't damage anything critical.

Success metric: Others handle the issue as well as—or better than—you would, and you don't feel the urge to intervene when problems arise in that domain.

Move 3: The Thinking Partnership (Builder Capability)

Start this month.

Train people to think through problems with you, not just report them.

Framework:

- **Welcome problems openly:** "I want to hear about every important issue, whether you have a solution or not."
- **Add thinking partnership:** "Let's work through this so you can handle it next time."
- **Ask:** "What have you considered so far? What options do you see?"
- **Guide discovery:** "What information would help? Who else has faced this?"
- **Build capability:** "Next time you see this, what would you try first?"
- **Notice the language shift:** Are they asking, "What do you want me to do?" (follower) or saying, "Here's what I think we should do because . . ." (member)?

For unsolved problems, partner with them. For solved ones, validate their thinking and expand learning. Over time, the majority of issues get handled without you—and people start thinking like members of the mission rather than followers of your direction.

Quick Start Implementation Plan

WEEK 1: START IMMEDIATELY

- Apply the ten-minute prevention reflex to every problem that lands on your desk.
- Track which problem categories recur most frequently.
- Pick *one* recurring category to systematize by the end of the week.

WEEK 2: BUILD YOUR FIRST SYSTEM

- Run the Netflix test: Identify what breaks first without you.
- Create the decision framework, authority matrix, or process guide that eliminates that dependency.
- Test it in a low-stakes situation this week.

MONTH 1: EXPAND AND VALIDATE

- Apply thinking-partnership coaching to five-plus situations.
- Measure: Are people bringing you solutions instead of just problems?
- Document what's working and refine your first system based on real results.

What's Not in the Fast Track

These three moves address your biggest bottlenecks immediately. But sustainable transformation requires what we haven't covered yet:

- **Identity transformation** (chapters 1, 9): Why your success patterns work against you, and how to rewire the psychological drivers that keep you in hero mode even when you know better
- **Advanced system design** (chapters 2, 5, 12): How to build systems that not only work without you, but improve without you—creating compound organizational intelligence
- **Membership architecture** (chapter 4): Why people follow your direction but don't act like owners, and how to design experiences that transform followers into members
- **Sustainability frameworks** (chapters 6–8, 10, 11): How to make architectural leadership feel natural instead of forced, and how to build leaders who build systems instead of creating dependency
- **Complete Tool Kit** (appendix I): More than a dozen implementation tools for systematic diagnosis, design, and transformation

If these three moves work naturally and create visible improvement, the full framework will accelerate your transformation exponentially. If they feel forced or don't generate results, start with chapters 1 and 9 to build the mindset foundation first.

Integration with the Full Framework

These three moves directly address the three invisible forces:

- Move 1 builds systematic patterns that work when complexity exceeds your capacity (force 3).
- Move 2 creates systems that adapt faster than you can think (force 2).
- Move 3 develops others' capabilities so your success patterns enable rather than constrain (force 1).

Together, they help you build Controller, Builder, and Architect repertoire—the CBA model described in the introduction.

For deeper transformation:

- **Move 1 (prevention reflex):** Chapter 2 (systems thinking)
- **Move 2 (Netflix test):** Chapters 2, 5, 12 (building through others)
- **Move 3 (thinking partnership):** Chapter 11 (the delegation breakthrough)

A Moment of Choice

Up to this point, this book has focused on recognition: seeing how the very strengths that drove your success can, over time, begin to limit your organization and your own capacity.

What follows is different.

Part II is written for leaders who are willing to try leading differently—not perfectly, but deliberately. It assumes a willingness to experiment with giving up at least one familiar habit in order to build something that lasts longer than personal effort.

If that's not where you are right now, it's fine to pause here. Many leaders never move beyond recognition, and part I may already be enough to help you make sense of what you're experiencing.

If you continue, do so intentionally.

The chapters ahead are designed to be used, not just read. They ask you to test new ways of working, redesign how decisions move, and build systems that perform without depending on you.

When you're ready, continue.

PART II

WIDER: BUILDING WHAT OUTLASTS YOU

THE MIDDLE DIMENSION OF ARCHITECTURAL leadership is the easiest to fake: building wider. This requires transferring judgment over delegating tasks, designing connections over approving them, developing fluency across functions over commanding within one, and trusting the system over relying on your own response time. When you master the "wider" dimension, the organization stops waiting for you and starts moving without you.

- **WHERE YOU'VE BEEN:** You've recognized the Hero Trap and started thinking in systems. You're catching yourself before solving problems others could handle.
- **WHERE YOU'RE GOING:** From individual capability to organizational capability. From "I solve" to "We solve better than I could alone."
- **CHAPTERS 5–8** help you build through others, create network effects, develop cross-functional fluency, and design stakeholder alignment.
- **YOU'RE READY FOR PART III WHEN:** Your team solves a problem you didn't anticipate, using principles you established but methods you never taught.

CHAPTER 5

From Doing to Designing

Building Through Others

Eyes on, hands off leadership

Alex thought delegation would buy him time. Then he looked at his calendar for the week and saw the truth: Maya wanted input on the road map, sales wanted him on the enterprise pricing call, engineering wanted him to break a tie on technical debt, customer success wanted him to join a renewal risk meeting. Different people, different topics—all the hard calls still boomeranged back to him.

He hadn't kept the work; he'd kept the *judgment.*

That was the moment he realized that unless he could transfer how he thought—not just what he decided—he'd always be the ceiling.

The Capacity Ceiling Problem

Reed Hastings faced an impossible problem in 2007. Netflix was growing explosively—from one million to twenty million subscribers—but every strategic decision still flowed through him personally. Content acquisition, technology priorities, international expansion, competitive responses. His calendar was booked solid with choices that "only the CEO could make."

The math was unforgiving: Effort alone couldn't scale what was structurally constrained. Rowing faster doesn't widen the river. He could work harder, hire more people to filter decisions, or fundamentally change how leadership worked at Netflix.

Hastings discovered a fundamental shift: from maximizing individual capacity to designing organizational systems that scale beyond any individual's capabilities.

At ParagonCX, Alex was discovering the same truth. His strength as a product visionary had fueled the company's early wins, but every new hire seemed to create more work for him, not less. The more capable people he added, the more they came to him for decisions. The math no longer worked: individual brilliance couldn't scale to meet collective complexity.

The Controller's Dilemma: When Individual Excellence Limits Team Potential

Most leaders start as Controllers in building through others because the Controller identity drove their individual success. You were promoted because you delivered results personally—solving problems, making decisions, executing excellently.

CONTROLLER BUILDING-THROUGH-OTHERS PATTERN

- "I'll handle the complex work and give you the simpler pieces."
- "Let me show you exactly how I would do this."
- "Check with me before proceeding on anything important."
- "I need to review this before it goes out."

This feels responsible and effective because it maintains quality while including others. But Controller building creates dependency, not capability.

The recognition moment: A team can't grow beyond its container. When your team's performance ceiling becomes your personal capacity ceiling, you've reached the limits of the Controller building-through-others pattern.

This is the Hero Trap from the introduction, now visible in how you build teams. Individual capacity scales linearly; organizational complexity scales exponentially. Building through others is how leaders escape it.

Building Through Others: From Alex's Decisions to Team Intelligence

Two years into his architectural transformation, with ParagonCX now at 120 employees, Alex decided it was time to let go.

He'd been the bottleneck on product decisions for too long. Maya—brilliant, strategic, the best product mind he'd ever worked with—deserved full ownership of the road map. So he gave it to her. "It's yours," he told her in their Monday one-on-one. "No more routing through me. You make the calls."

He felt good about it. Architect-like. He cleared three recurring meetings from his calendar and spent the week on strategic planning for the first time in months.

Three weeks later, he sat in a client review, watching it unravel.

Whitfield Medical—their second-largest enterprise account—had flown in for a quarterly business review. Maya had restructured the road map around mid-market customers, which made sense from a product standpoint. What she hadn't seen was that Whitfield's integration timeline depended on two features she'd deprioritized. Their VP of operations, David Whitfield himself, was looking at a slide showing those features pushed to Q4.

"I was told these would be ready by August," Whitfield said. His voice was even. The kind of even that took effort.

Maya handled it well—she explained the reasoning, offered alternatives, stayed composed. But Alex watched Whitfield's face as she talked. Not angry. Recalculating. Deciding whether ParagonCX was still the right bet.

After the meeting, Alex walked Maya to her office. She knew.

"I didn't have the full picture," she said. "I didn't know Whitfield's integration depended on those features. I made the call based on what I could see."

Alex opened his mouth to reassure her—and stopped. Because the problem wasn't Maya. The problem was him. He'd handed her the keys and kept the map in his desk drawer. She'd made decisions with 20 percent of the information he carried around in his head. Of course those decisions looked disconnected from strategy. She couldn't see what he'd never shared.

He'd delegated the task without transferring the judgment. Authority without context. Responsibility without capability.

Delegation isn't giving someone your work. It's giving them your *thinking*. And Alex had never done that. He'd only ever given people his conclusions.

What Alex learned through trial and error was that building others' capability required understanding both the technical progression and the psychological barriers that make delegation feel threatening to everyone involved.

The same forces from the introduction—success patterns, BANI conditions, systems complexity—were creating predictable psychological barriers.

The Psychological Barriers to Building Through Others

Why do so many leaders struggle to transition from individual contribution to building others? Three psychological barriers consistently emerge:

- **The expert identity:** "I'm valued for my expertise and problem-solving ability." This pulls you into the Hero Trap. But expertise limits organizational capability when broader skills are needed.
- **The control illusion:** "If I'm not directly involved, quality will suffer." But quality then tops out at your personal capacity and review speed.
- **The indispensability addiction:** "Being needed proves my value." But indispensability constrains growth and reduces your strategic impact.

Understanding the Resistance

Before Alex could delegate effectively, he had to recognize why it felt wrong to both of them. His own resistance was subtle but real: "If Maya can make these strategic decisions, what makes me valuable?" Part of him worried that developing her too much might make him replaceable. Another part felt guilty about "working less" while she took on more responsibility.

Maya's resistance was different but equally understandable. She worried that taking full product authority might set her up to fail publicly, threatening her reputation for competence. She also genuinely cared about customer outcomes and feared that her decisions might hurt people if she got things wrong.

"I realized that what looked like 'resistance to change' was really values-based concern about what delegation meant," Alex said later. "Maya wasn't avoiding responsibility—she was protecting things she cared about."

The Context Foundation

Alex's breakthrough came when he addressed these concerns while sharing his reasoning. Instead of saying "prioritize the enterprise features," he explained the customer segments driving revenue, the competitive landscape pressuring their positioning, the technology constraints limiting options, and the financial models determining viability.

But he also positioned the authority transfer as recognition of Maya's expertise rather than replacement of his own. "You understand customer needs better than anyone," he told her. "I want you to apply that insight to strategic decisions, not just feature specifications."

"I realized Maya was making decisions with 20 percent of the information I had," Alex said. "No wonder her choices seemed disconnected from strategy—she couldn't see what I was seeing."

Within weeks of receiving this context, Maya began making aligned decisions without Alex's constant input. She wasn't replicating his choices—she was applying his strategic thinking to situations he'd never encountered.

Building Decision Judgment

But context alone wasn't enough. Maya still called Alex whenever decisions felt complex or risky. So Alex shifted from providing answers to teaching principles while creating safety nets that addressed her deeper concerns.

He walked Maya through how he weighed customer impact against strategic alignment, how he balanced resource efficiency with learning velocity, how he evaluated short-term wins against long-term positioning. But he also set clear escalation criteria: "If a decision could affect customer renewal rates or could require budget changes over $50k, bring me in. Otherwise, you have full authority."

"Instead of telling Maya what to decide, I taught her how I think about decisions," Alex explained. "She learned to ask the same questions I ask, consider the same trade-offs I consider. And she knew I had her back if something went wrong."

Maya's decision quality improved dramatically, but more importantly, her confidence grew. The guardrails Alex had created meant she could take authority without feeling like she was risking customer harm or her own reputation.

Handing Over Decisions

The real test came when Alex created what Maya called the "traffic light system." Green decisions Maya made independently. Yellow decisions she made but informed Alex afterward. Red decisions they made together.

On paper, it was elegant. In practice, it almost broke them.

Three weeks after launching the system, Maya walked into Alex's office and closed the door. Her jaw was tight.

"We need to talk about the Meridian feature decision."

Alex looked up from his laptop. "What about it? You made the call—that was a green-zone decision."

"I made the call," Maya said. "And then you had a side conversation with Chen about 'refining the technical approach.' Which changed the scope. Which delayed the timeline. Which meant I had to go back to the customer and revise the commitment I'd already made."

Alex opened his mouth to explain.

"This is the third time," Maya continued. "The third time you've said 'green zone' and then quietly walked it back through a side channel. I'm not asking you to agree with every call I make. I'm asking you to be honest about what you're actually willing to let go of."

The words hung in the air.

"Because right now," she said, "you're teaching me that 'I trust you' means 'I trust you until I don't.' And that's worse than just making the decisions yourself. At least then I'd know where I stand."

Alex sat with that for a long moment. His first instinct was to defend himself—he'd just been offering perspective, helping Chen think through implications, not overruling Maya. But he replayed the last three weeks and saw it the way she saw it: a pattern of public delegation and private revision.

"You're right," he said finally. "I've been delegating the words while keeping the control."

Maya's shoulders dropped slightly. "I don't need you to be perfect. I need you to be consistent. If it's green, let it be green. If you're not ready for that, make it yellow. But don't put me in front of customers with authority you're going to undermine."

Alex realized he'd been running two systems: the official traffic light and an invisible shadow system where he still shaped outcomes through "suggestions" and "context" that everyone knew to treat as direction. Maya had called it what it was.

The next week, Alex did something harder than delegating: He watched Maya make a decision he disagreed with and said nothing. The feature launched. Customer feedback was positive. His way would have worked too—but hers wasn't wrong. It was just different.

That was when the traffic light system became real.

"The genius wasn't the categories," Maya reflected later. "It was that Alex finally stopped hedging. Once he committed—really committed—decision speed tripled because I wasn't waiting for his approval on things I could handle myself. And because I wasn't spending half my energy managing around his second-guessing."

The system worked because it honored both of their values.

Maya got authority that felt like recognition rather than risk. Alex maintained strategic involvement without becoming a bottleneck. Within three months, 80 percent of product decisions were happening in Maya's green zone.

Alex's calendar freed up for the strategic work he'd been putting off for months. More importantly, Maya was making some decisions better than Alex would have—she was closer to customer feedback and had fresher perspectives on technical possibilities.

When Others Start Teaching

Six months into this transformation, something unexpected happened. Maya began teaching Alex's frameworks to junior product managers. She documented the decision-making processes, created templates for competitive analysis, and mentored engineers on thinking strategically about technical trade-offs.

"Maya wasn't just using the capability I'd transferred to her," Alex observed. "She was multiplying it throughout the organization. Knowledge was spreading naturally instead of being bottlenecked through me."

When a new product manager joined the team, Maya onboarded them using the same systematic approach Alex had used with her—including the same attention to psychological safety and values-based concerns. The new hire reached independence faster than anyone Alex had personally developed because Maya had improved on his original frameworks.

How Alex's Identity Changed

Looking back, Alex realized his own identity had evolved through this process.

"As a Controller, I was solving Maya's strategic challenges through personal involvement. When she needed product direction, I provided answers. When conflicts arose, I mediated. I was the solution, which made me the bottleneck.

"As a Builder, I taught Maya the frameworks I used for product strategy. I shared customer insights, competitive analysis approaches, and decision-making principles. She learned to think using my methods, but she still needed me to guide complex situations.

"As an Architect, I designed systems that gave Maya the context, authority, and frameworks to make strategic decisions independently. The systems enabled her success without requiring my ongoing involvement—while honoring both our concerns about what effective delegation actually means."

The progression was clear: hands on everything as a Controller, hands coaching as a Builder, and finally eyes on, hands off as an Architect. Alex maintained visibility into product strategy and outcomes—he knew what was happening and could spot patterns—but his hands were off the daily decisions and execution. Maya didn't need his approval; she needed his architecture.

That's the shift from Controller to Architect.

The transformation revealed something profound about organizational capability: When people understand not just what to do but why and how to think about decisions—and when they feel safe to exercise that judgment—they don't just execute better, they innovate beyond what the original leader could have imagined.

A year later, Maya's product organization was generating strategic insights Alex had never considered, solving customer problems he hadn't identified, and building competitive advantages he couldn't have designed alone. The symphony had become more capable than its conductor.

How Systems Build Trust Faster

Most leaders believe trust must develop slowly through personal relationships. But Alex discovered that Architect leadership in building through others accelerates trust through systematic transparency and capability development.

Alex's breakthrough with Maya wasn't about building personal trust over months—it was about designing systems that made trust logical and immediate.

After that missed release, Alex didn't give a trust-building speech. Instead, he shared his decision record, showing exactly where his judgment failed and what he'd check differently next time. He committed to specific process changes and followed through consistently. He celebrated people who improved the system, not just those who delivered features.

Trust emerged because Maya could see Alex's thinking, predict his responses, and count on systematic follow-through rather than hoping for personal consistency.

Alex's experience with Maya highlights a deeper truth: The quality of a leader's systems depends on the quality of the people shaping them.

Covering Blind Spots

Don't just design for functional coverage—design for *cognitive coverage*. Surround yourself with leaders who believe in the mission but think differently enough to sharpen your judgment, including the courage to disagree. If two executives bring essentially the same worldview, skills, and experiences, one is redundant. When a needed perspective is missing, supplement the team with an *advisory council* (internal or external) so those voices reliably shape your most important decisions.

But even the best team can't compensate for a leader who's still doing the work instead of designing how it gets done.

The Brutal Truth Test

Look at your calendar from last week. How many hours were spent on work that someone else could have done if you'd invested two to three hours in building their capability or creating a system? Table 1 shows the annual cost of work that could have been delegated or systematized.

TABLE 1: Hidden Capacity Cost

Hours/week on transferable work	Annual capacity loss
5 hours	250 hours (6 weeks)
10 hours	500 hours (12 weeks)
15 hours	750 hours (19 weeks)
20 hours	1,000 hours (25 weeks)

If you're in the ten-to-fifteen-hour range, you're losing a full quarter of your year to work that shouldn't reach you. Not because you're bad at delegating. Because being needed feels better than being free.

For the complete 2-Week Calendar Audit that reveals your actual Controller/Builder/Architect pattern, see the Building Through Others Assessment in appendix I (access the appendices at catalystgrowthadvisors.com/the-hero-trap/*).*

Your Next Move This Week

Pick one area where people currently depend on your personal involvement.

Start small: Choose something that happens weekly and matters to the outcome but doesn't risk catastrophic failure if it goes wrong.

Your goal is to shift from hands on to eyes on, hands off. You'll still know what's happening. You're not disappearing, but you're building systems that give you visibility without requiring your constant involvement.

APPLY ALEX'S PROGRESSION:

1. **Share your reasoning** (not just your conclusion).
2. **Teach the principles** you use to make these decisions.
3. **Create clear boundaries** for when they should involve you versus proceed independently.
4. **Step back and observe** what happens.

The test: Can this work well during your next vacation?

Example: Instead of approving every customer proposal, teach your frameworks for pricing and risk assessment, then create dollar thresholds that determine approval authority.

What Success Looks Like

You'll know you're building through others effectively when the following occurs:

- People stop asking, "What do you want me to do?" and start saying, "Here's what I think we should do because . . ."

- Your calendar has more strategic time because fewer decisions wait for your input.
- Team members teach each other approaches you originally taught them.
- Solutions emerge that you wouldn't have thought of yourself.

The goal isn't to become unnecessary—it's to become strategically essential rather than operationally critical. Your value shifts from having the answers to building people who can find better answers than you would alone.

When Maya started generating product insights Alex had never considered, he realized he'd achieved something more valuable than personal expertise: He'd created organizational intelligence that exceeded his individual capacity.

Design Beats Default: Why Systematic Delegation Scales

Alex's transformation with respect to Maya demonstrates why design beats default in leadership development. Most managers default to either micromanagement ("I'll stay involved to ensure quality") or hope-based delegation ("Just figure it out and let me know if you need help"). Both approaches create inconsistent results that depend entirely on the manager's personal skills and availability.

But when other leaders at ParagonCX saw Alex's systematic approach producing better results—faster decisions, higher quality outcomes, more engaged team members—they began copying his frameworks rather than continuing to rely on intuition.

DEFAULT DELEGATION:

- happens when workload forces you to hand things off
- relies on the leader's personal relationship skills and gut instincts
- varies wildly in effectiveness based on individual leadership style
- dies when that leader leaves or gets overwhelmed

DESIGNED DELEGATION:

- follows systematic frameworks for context, authority, and capability transfer
- generates consistent results regardless of leadership personality
- can be documented, taught, and improved over time
- spreads naturally as other leaders see the effectiveness

This is how organizational capability scales: through designed systems that multiple people can implement, not heroic approaches that only work for the original creator. When your colleagues observe you systematically building others' capabilities and retaining top performers, they don't just admire the outcomes—they want to understand the system.

Alex's delegation frameworks became organizationally viral because they were architecture, not artistry. Other managers could implement the same systematic approach and achieve similar results, regardless of their natural coaching intuition or relationship-building skills.

From Hero Teams to Architect Systems

Building great teams is necessary. It's also not enough.

Consider two leaders who transformed organizations at the highest possible stakes—and notice where each one lands on the Controller ➔ Builder ➔ Architect progression.

Bill Campbell, the legendary Silicon Valley coach, helped build Apple, Google, and Intuit by doing something deceptively simple: He made the people in the room better. He surfaced tensions executives wouldn't name, coached leaders through their blind spots, paired people who didn't naturally trust each other, and insisted that teams work on the team first, then the problem. The results were extraordinary. The companies he touched generated over a trillion dollars in market value.[1]

But Campbell's approach had a signature limitation: It required Bill Campbell. He sat in on executive meetings. He coached one-on-one. He read the room and intervened in real time. When he died in 2016, the people he'd coached mourned not just a friend but an irreplaceable capability. His genius was Builder genius—"I show how I solve"—applied at the highest level. He created hero teams: brilliant people, working brilliantly together, still anchored to an extraordinary individual.

General Stanley McChrystal faced a different problem—and arrived at a different solution. When he took command of the Joint Special Operations Command (JSOC) in Iraq, he had the most elite small teams on earth. Navy SEALs, Delta Force, Army Rangers—each unit operated with extraordinary trust and shared purpose. But at the organizational level, these teams couldn't coordinate fast enough to match an enemy that moved like a network while JSOC still operated like a hierarchy. McChrystal's insight wasn't to coach the teams harder. It was to redesign the architecture connecting them.

He built two systems: shared consciousness—so everyone understood the whole picture, not just their part—and empowered execution—so decisions happened where the information lived, not where the authority sat. Then he did something that reveals the Architect identity at its core: He designed himself out of the loop. He admitted that being woken at 2 a.m. for life-and-death decisions made him feel important and needed—and then recognized that his approval wasn't producing better decisions, just slower ones.[2]

Campbell made leaders better. McChrystal made the system smarter. Campbell's teams needed him in the room. McChrystal's organization could survive the loss of anyone—including McChrystal.

Both were transformational. But only one scales beyond the leader's presence.

The environment most leaders operate in today looks far more like McChrystal's Iraq than Campbell's Silicon Valley. The question isn't whether you can build a great team. It's whether you can design systems that make great teams possible without you.

Alex was about to find out he'd already started.

Six months after Alex's breakthrough with Maya, something unexpected happened. Other team leaders at ParagonCX started asking him how his people had become so capable of working together across departments. They'd noticed that Maya's team wasn't just independent—they were connecting with engineering, sales, and customer success in ways that created solutions no single department could have generated alone. Alex realized he'd accidentally discovered something more powerful than building through others: building others who build networks. But scaling that kind of connected intelligence across an entire organization? That would require a completely different kind of architecture.

The Point of No Return

This isn't a dramatic moment.

There's no announcement, no reorganization, no visible shift. The point of no return happens quietly, when you choose one decision you've always made and decide that you won't make it anymore.

From that moment on, leadership stops being about stepping in and starts being about designing what carries judgment forward without you.

Choose one category of decisions that currently routes to you by default. Not the most critical decisions. Not the ones that truly require your judgment. Choose a category where your involvement has become habitual rather than essential.

If you're not sure where to start, leaders often begin with decisions like these:

- prioritizing work or sequencing tasks
- approving routine spending below a set threshold
- resolving internal trade-offs between teams
- deciding how work is staffed or handed off
- setting standards for quality or completion

Choose one that currently finds its way to you out of habit, not necessity.

For the next ninety days, make this commitment: **You will not make these decisions.**

Instead:

- You will clarify what a good decision looks like.
- You will name who owns the decision.
- You will design the information and boundaries they need to decide well.

If the system fails, resist the urge to step back in. Redesign the system rather than reclaiming the decision.

This is not about withdrawal or abdication. It's about shifting where leadership lives.

Make this commitment visible. Tell your team what you're doing and why. Let them know this is an experiment, not a test of loyalty or competence.

At the end of ninety days, decide what to keep, what to adjust, and what to take back. But don't decide early. The discomfort is part of the data.

You don't become an Architect by doing less.

You become an Architect by refusing to rescue work the system should be able to carry.

The Signal Box

Delegation isn't giving someone your work—it's giving them your thinking.

Key insights from this chapter:

- Authority without context creates failure; responsibility without capability creates resentment.
- The progression is hands on (Controller), hands coaching (Builder), and finally eyes on, hands off (Architect).
- Public delegation paired with private revision teaches your team that "I trust you" means "I trust you until I don't."
- Designed delegation scales because it can be documented, taught, and improved; default delegation dies with the leader who invented it.
- Building through others is how leaders escape the math of complexity that no individual capacity can match.

When the people you've developed start improving on your frameworks and teaching them to others, you've built capability that compounds without you.

> **If you remember only one thing: You haven't delegated until they can decide without you—and decide well.**

Learning Prompt

When you imagine your team making 80 percent of the right decisions without you, what makes you excited about that possibility? What makes you nervous?

Both feelings are pointing to something real. This week, design one small experiment that tests whether collective decision-making works in your specific context.

The curiosity: You might discover that your team's combined judgment exceeds your individual expertise in ways that surprise you—or you might learn what conditions need to exist first.

CHAPTER 6

Network Effects

Creating Connections That Scale

Teams that evolve together, resolve together.

Alex Chen stared at the Slack thread and felt his temples throb. Eleven p.m. on a Wednesday. Again. Marcus from sales and Chen from engineering were locked in what looked like agreement but felt like miscommunication.

Marcus: "The enterprise client needs this production ready by Q2."

Chen: "We can absolutely ship something by Q2 if we skip the technical debt work."

Alex's fingers hovered over the keyboard. The dopamine hit was predictable—he'd translate, they'd understand, the crisis would resolve. He'd done this exact dance dozens of times in the past quarter.

But this time, he noticed something he'd never let himself see before.

He was looking forward to it.

Not the problem. Not the late hour. Not the miscommunication that would cost them days if left unresolved. He was looking forward to *being the one who fixed it*. There was a small, shameful flutter of anticipation in his chest—the feeling of being needed, of being essential, of being the only person who could bridge this gap.

I'm excited about this.

The thought was clear enough that he couldn't pretend it away. Somewhere beneath the exhaustion, beneath the frustration at another 11 p.m. crisis, part of him was *relieved* that the system had broken. Relieved that the hero was required. Relieved that his value was about to be proven, one more time.

He remembered something a therapist had told him years ago, back when he still made time for therapy: "Pay attention to what you reach for when you're anxious. That's usually the addiction talking."

Alex looked at the phone in his hand. The cursor blinking in the Slack window.

This is the addiction talking.

The realization didn't stop him. His fingers were already moving: "What Marcus means by 'production ready' is . . ."

But this time, he felt the hit when he pressed send. The small chemical reward for being indispensable. The microdose of significance that came from being the answer.

He'd never noticed it before because he'd never wanted to. Noticing meant admitting that his exhaustion wasn't entirely imposed on him. That some part of him had been *choosing* this—choosing to be needed over choosing to build something that didn't need him.

His hands froze above the keys.

He'd written a version of that sentence dozens of times. Not because sales couldn't learn it. Because he'd never made it *easier than going through him*. He hadn't just fixed misalignment—he'd trained the whole company to route it to him.

His stomach clenched. Not with anxiety—with recognition.

How many times have I explained what "scalable" means to sales? When did I become the universal translator?

He opened his calendar analytics. The data was devastating:

- eighteen hours per week in "alignment meetings"
- 67 percent of those meetings: him translating between departments
- same issues, same people, recurring monthly

Six months ago, he'd celebrated Maya's transformation. She'd become independent, even teaching others his frameworks. He'd solved the vertical problem—building capability within teams.

But *between* functions? Every coordination point still flowed through him.

He was the bottleneck he'd designed himself out of everywhere else.

Sales spoke revenue metrics and customer promises. Engineering spoke technical specifications and system constraints. Product spoke user experiences and feature priorities. Finance spoke cash flow and unit economics.

Each function was brilliant individually. Together, they couldn't coordinate a simple customer request without his translation.

The First Attempt

The next morning, Alex decided to fix it.

"Marcus, Chen—you two need to work this out directly. I'm not scheduling another translation meeting."

He felt virtuous. Empowering. Architect-like.

Three days later, the enterprise deal was in jeopardy.

Marcus, eager to close: "We can turn around the legacy integration in six to eight weeks."

Chen, hearing about it later: "That's impossible without rebuilding our entire API. Maybe six months if we delay everything else."

Product, caught in the middle: "Could work if we scope it differently, but nobody asked why the customer actually needs this."

Finance, reviewing afterward: "We can't afford a six-month custom project regardless."

The customer, frustrated by conflicting information, went with a competitor.

The call Alex made to Patricia Okonkwo at Nexfield was the worst part.

"I wanted to call personally to—"

"To explain why your sales team promised something your engineering team couldn't deliver?" She didn't sound angry. She sounded tired. "We picked you over two larger vendors because you seemed different. More personal." She paused. "I guess 'personal' just meant everything ran through you. And when it didn't, nothing worked."

He had no response. She was exactly right.

"I hope you figure it out," she said. "But we can't wait while you do."

Alex sat with his hand on the phone. Patricia hadn't been angry. She'd been disappointed—in him specifically, in what he'd built. Somehow that was worse.

Jordan from customer success appeared at his office door.

"Not now." The words came out harder than Alex intended.

"It's time sensitive. I'm seeing the same pattern we just . . ."

"I said not now." Alex didn't look up from his screen. "Handle it. That's literally what I pay you for."

The silence lasted three seconds.

When Alex finally glanced up, Jordan's face had gone carefully blank—the professional mask people wear when they've just learned something about their boss they can't unlearn.

"Of course. Sorry to interrupt."

The door closed softly.

Alex's stomach dropped. He'd seen that exact expression on people's faces before—usually right before they updated their LinkedIn profiles.

When did I become the kind of leader people have to manage around?

He thought about going after Jordan to apologize. Instead, he sat there, shame pooling in his chest, telling himself he'd make it right tomorrow. That's what exhausted people do. They defer the hard conversations and hope the damage isn't permanent.

I told them to collaborate directly and they blew up a major deal. See? They need me to translate.

But that night, he couldn't sleep.

The Intervention

Maya found him the next morning staring at his laptop in the conference room.

"You've been here since 6 a.m.," she said carefully. "What's wrong?"

"I tried to get sales and engineering to work together directly. It was a disaster."

"Can I tell you what I've noticed?" She sat down across from him. "Within my product team, people coordinate brilliantly without me.

But the moment we need to work with sales or engineering, everything routes through you."

Alex felt defensive. "I'm just helping with coordination—"

"You're not coordinating," Maya interrupted gently. "You're translating. And we're not learning the language."

"What am I supposed to do—just let functions misunderstand each other and blow deals?"

"No," Maya said. "But you're solving the symptom, not the system. You increased my independence six months ago by designing systems that transferred capability. You didn't just tell me to 'figure it out'—you gave me context, frameworks, authority, and safety."

She stood to leave, then turned back.

"What if functions need the same thing? Not just permission to collaborate, but systems that make collaboration easier than going through you?"

• • • •

Alex wasn't coordinating—he was translating. And every translation taught the organization that it couldn't speak for itself.

Alex couldn't sleep that night. Maya's words kept replaying.

Systems that make collaboration easier than going through you.

He remembered something he'd read years ago—a quote from Antoine de Saint-Exupéry: "If you want to build a ship, don't drum up the men to gather wood, divide the work, and give orders. Instead, teach them to yearn for the vast and endless sea."

But Alex realized yearning wasn't enough. In complex organizations, you need systems that help people find each other, combine their capabilities, and create value together. Systems beat heroics because individual knowledge has limits while network intelligence compounds infinitely.

His research led him to Reid Hoffman, who'd built LinkedIn on this exact principle. Hoffman discovered that the platform's value wasn't in the individual profiles—it was in the connections between them. A single profile was just information. But when profiles connected, they created network effects: Each new connection made the entire platform more valuable for everyone.

Hoffman realized that the same principle applied to organizations. Individual expertise was limited by personal capacity, but connected expertise could create exponential value through what he called "network intelligence"—capabilities that emerged from people working together in ways no individual could achieve alone.

But Hoffman noticed something crucial: Network effects didn't happen automatically. They required intentional architecture. Random connections created noise, not value. Valuable networks emerged from systematic design that made collaboration easier, safer, and more rewarding than individual effort.

This insight led to one of the most powerful organizational transformations in Silicon Valley history: LinkedIn's internal "small world network" approach that enabled sixteen thousand employees to function like a start-up while delivering at a Fortune 500 scale.[1]

Alex kept reading. LinkedIn's transformation proved that network intelligence creates extraordinary organizational capabilities. But if the benefits were so compelling, why did he—and most leaders—still default to individual thinking and centralized control?

The answer, he discovered, lay in how our brains are wired to resist the very collaboration that creates network effects.

Your Brain Undervalues Networks

The same neural wiring that made you an effective individual contributor now works against the network intelligence your role demands.

Evolutionary psychology explains why leaders default to individual thinking: For thousands of years, human survival depended on personal competence and small-group coordination. Our brains are wired to trust what we can control directly.

The SCARF Barriers to Network Thinking

Our brains' resistance to networks follows predictable patterns. Neuroscientist David Rock's SCARF model identifies five domains where social threats trigger the *same* neural response as physical threats:[2]

- **Status:** Sharing expertise might diminish personal competitive advantage.

- **Certainty:** Network outcomes feel less controllable than individual results.
- **Autonomy:** Collaboration requires interdependence that reduces personal control.
- **Relatedness:** Network value depends on others' participation and contribution.
- **Fairness:** Value creation and credit distribution become complex.

At ParagonCX, Alex experienced this resistance firsthand.

It started with a customer escalation six months earlier. Sarah from engineering had the technical answer. Marcus from sales understood the customer relationship. The logical solution: Put them on the call together.

Alex bristled at the thought.

What if Sarah gets too technical and confuses them? What if Marcus promises something we can't deliver?

- **Status:** If they could solve customer issues without him, what made him valuable?
- **Certainty:** He could predict outcomes when he controlled the conversation. Direct collaboration felt chaotic.
- **Autonomy:** Letting them work together meant accepting he couldn't control the result.
- **Relatedness:** His relationships with both teams depended on being the trusted intermediary.
- **Fairness:** Who would get credit if the collaboration succeeded?

So Alex joined the call. Translated between technical and business language. Solved the immediate problem. Maintained his role as the essential connector.

The pattern repeated weekly for months.

He told himself he was being responsible. Protecting quality. Ensuring customer success.

But Maya's words kept echoing: *You're not coordinating. You're translating. And we're not learning the language.*

Alex finally understood: His brain wasn't protecting the company. It was protecting him from the perceived threats of letting go. The SCARF barriers weren't logical. They were neurological. His resistance felt like wisdom but was actually fear wearing a disguise.

Only when he designed systems that made collaboration predictable and accountable did those anxieties fade. The network began to outperform his individual judgment.

Stop optimizing your hiring process for individual IQ and start designing your collaboration systems. The smartest hire in the world won't save you if your team's interaction patterns are broken. But average hires with excellent collaboration architecture will consistently outperform your competitors' genius teams.

The Architect insight: Your job isn't to be the smartest person in the room. It's to design the room so it's collectively smarter than any individual, including you.

When the room is designed to be smarter than you, your absence doesn't lower the ceiling. That's the difference between heroic leadership and architectural leadership. One depends on the leader's presence, the other depends on the system's design.

The Failed Experiments

Three months after the blown enterprise deal, Alex committed to testing direct collaboration systematically.

Experiment 1: Random Connections

Alex created Slack channels for cross-functional collaboration: #product-eng-collab, #sales-success-sync, #all-hands-ideas.

Week one: 847 messages. Week four: 23 messages. Week eight: Crickets.

People joined enthusiastically but then stopped participating. The channels filled with noise—updates no one needed, questions that went unanswered, ideas that died in the thread.

Alex's neck muscles tensed as he scrolled through the dead channels.

> **Random connections don't create value. They create obligation without benefit.**

Experiment 2: Forced Collaboration

Alex tried the opposite. New policy: Sales and engineering must collaborate on every deal over $50,000. Required joint calls. Mandatory handoffs. Structured check-ins.

Engineering groaned about sales calls wasting their time. Sales complained that engineering was blocking deals. Customer response times doubled.

Marcus cornered Alex after a particularly tense meeting. "This isn't working. We're collaborating more and delivering less."

Alex felt exhaustion settle into his shoulders. His fingers pressed into his temples.

> **Forced collaboration creates resentment, not results.**

That night, reviewing the failures, Alex realized his mistake. He'd been treating all connections as equal—assuming any collaboration was better than none. But random connections created noise. Forced connections created friction.

He needed to understand what made some connections valuable and others worthless.

His research led him back to LinkedIn's approach. Hoffman hadn't just enabled connections—he'd designed for specific types of network effects. Each type required different infrastructure, different incentives, different design.

Alex realized that not all connections create value. The question wasn't "Should people collaborate?" but "What types of connections create compound returns?"

The Four Types of Network Effects in Organizations

Not all connections create value. Architect leaders understand the difference between random networking and systematic network effects that compound over time. Most leaders treat networking as a personal activity. Architect leaders treat it as an organizational design challenge. Here are the four types of network effects in organizations:

TYPE 1: DIRECT NETWORK EFFECTS

- **What it is:** The value of participation increases directly with the number of participants.
- **Organizational example:** Slack channels become more valuable as more people join relevant conversations.
- **Design principle:** Make participation easy and immediately valuable.

TYPE 2: INDIRECT NETWORK EFFECTS

- **What it is:** Growth in one part of the network increases value in a different part.
- **Organizational example:** Sales team insights make product development more effective, which makes customer success easier, which generates better sales intelligence.
- **Design principle:** Create feedback loops between different functions.

TYPE 3: LEARNING NETWORK EFFECTS

- **What it is:** The system gets smarter as more people use it and contribute knowledge.
- **Organizational example:** Customer support documentation improves with each new case, making the entire support function more effective.
- **Design principle:** Capture and share learning automatically rather than relying on individual initiative.

TYPE 4: INNOVATION NETWORK EFFECTS

- **What it is:** Unexpected combinations of expertise create breakthrough innovations.

- **Organizational example:** Engineers working with customer success teams discover product improvements that neither function could envision alone.
- **Design principle:** Design serendipitous collisions between different types of expertise.

ParagonCX's evolution: Alex moved from trying to be the central hub of all knowledge to designing systems that enabled different combinations of expertise to create value automatically.

ParagonCX's Network Breakthrough

Eighteen months after the failed experiments, Alex faced the ultimate test.

A major enterprise customer—one that represented 12 percent of annual revenue—was experiencing integration issues that no single function could solve. The problem required the following:

- deep technical understanding of API architecture (engineering expertise)
- knowledge of the customer's industry-specific workflows (sales expertise)
- experience with similar integration patterns (customer success expertise)
- understanding of data security requirements (legal/compliance expertise)

The customer needed a solution in forty-eight hours or they'd escalate to cancellation.

Alex stared at his keyboard. His fingers hovered over the keys to schedule an emergency meeting.

I could solve this. Gather everyone, synthesize the inputs, design the solution. Like I always have.

His heart rate picked up. The familiar pull—the one he'd finally named. Being the one with answers.

But he caught himself.

That's Controller thinking. I built systems for this exact situation.

He opened Slack and watched.

Hours one through four: Engineering tagged the issue as #integrationcomplex. The system automatically suggested three people with relevant experience: Chen (engineering), Marcus (sales), and Jordan (customer success).

Within twenty minutes, they'd created a shared channel.

Alex watched uneasily. *Don't intervene. Trust the system.*

Hours four through twelve: The team analyzed requirements together. Chen explained the API constraints. Marcus shared the customer's actual workflow needs—not what they'd asked for, but what they were trying to accomplish. Jordan pulled patterns from two similar integrations they'd completed last quarter.

Alex watched the conversation unfold. His chest felt tight. *They're missing the security angle. Legal needs to be involved.*

But before he could type anything, Jordan @-mentioned legal: "We'll need security framework guidance here."

The system is working without me.

Hours twelve through twenty-four: Legal joined the thread and provided the compliance requirements directly to engineering. No translation through Alex. No delays waiting for his schedule.

The team started prototyping solutions. Not one solution—three different approaches, each addressing different aspects of the problem.

Alex's anxiety shifted to curiosity. *They're exploring possibilities I hadn't even considered.*

Hours twenty-four through thirty-six: The team narrowed their focus to one approach, but it was different from what Alex would have designed. It was better. They'd identified integration challenges he didn't even know existed because their collective intelligence exceeded his individual understanding.

By hour forty-eight, they presented their solution to the customer.

Alex joined the call to observe. He didn't speak.

The customer approved. Implementation timeline: three weeks instead of the six months Alex had assumed it would take.

After the call ended, Alex sat alone in the conference room. "Huh," he said to no one.

The organization had solved a critical problem he couldn't have solved alone. The network's intelligence exceeded his capacity. His absence hadn't lowered the ceiling—it had raised it.

He felt two emotions simultaneously:

Loss: *They don't need me to solve this anymore.*

Pride: *They solved it better than I could have.*

And then recognition: *This is what I built Maya's capability for—but at organizational scale.*

As a Controller, he would have been the solution—gathering inputs, synthesizing information, making the final decision. The organization would have been limited by his capacity and judgment.

As a Builder, he would have taught them his approach to integration problems. They would have learned his methods but stayed dependent on his frameworks.

As an Architect, he had designed systems that enabled the organization to produce solutions he couldn't conceive. The systems worked without him. More importantly, they worked *better* without him because collective intelligence exceeded individual capacity.

The network had proven itself. And Alex had finally escaped the Hero Trap.

The Trust Velocity Challenge

The biggest barrier to network effects isn't technology—it's trust. People won't share knowledge or seek help unless they feel psychologically safe and confident that contribution will be valued.

Amy Edmondson's research on psychological safety reveals four progressive stages that enable network intelligence:[3]

STAGE 1: INCLUSION SAFETY

- People feel safe to be themselves and belong to the network.
- Design elements: Clear membership criteria, welcoming onboarding, visible diversity of participants

STAGE 2: LEARNER SAFETY

- People feel safe to ask questions and admit what they don't know.
- Design elements: "No stupid questions" policies, reward systems for curiosity, leaders modeling learning behavior

STAGE 3: CONTRIBUTOR SAFETY

- People feel safe to share ideas and expertise without fear of criticism.
- Design elements: Constructive feedback protocols, recognition for contribution, protection from idea theft

STAGE 4: CHALLENGER SAFETY

- People feel safe to question assumptions and suggest better approaches.
- Design elements: Systematic encouragement of different perspectives, rewards for productive dissent, conflict resolution systems

ParagonCX's trust acceleration: Alex didn't wait for trust to develop naturally. He designed specific practices that moved people through all four safety stages systematically, reducing the time from initial connection to productive collaboration.

BUILDING NETWORK CONFIDENCE (QUICK VERSION)

- **Notice it:** Pay attention to when collaboration delivers better results than you could achieve alone.
- **Test it:** Try a "connection experiment": Instead of solving a problem, connect two people and step back.
- **Design it:** Build one small system that makes collaboration happen without you.
- **Recognize it:** Spot when those systems create results no individual could achieve.

The Signal Box

Network effects don't just improve coordination—they create intelligence that emerges from connections between people.

Key insights from this chapter:

- Heroes optimize individuals; Architects optimize interactions.
- Systems beat heroics because network intelligence scales exponentially while individual intelligence scales linearly.
- Value doesn't just add up—it multiplies through well-designed connections.
- The goal isn't better knowledge management—it's emergent organizational intelligence.

When your organization starts solving problems no individual taught it to solve, you've created network intelligence.

> **If you remember only one thing: You're either the bridge people need or the bottleneck they're stuck behind.**

Learning Prompt

Some of the best solutions I've seen come from unexpected connections between people with different expertise. But making those connections happen consistently is harder than it looks.

Pick that person on your team who has expertise others could benefit from. Before creating any connections, think: What usually prevents valuable knowledge from flowing directly between people who need each other?

This week, create one simple way for others to find that person directly instead of going through you. Pay attention to what happens—both what works and what doesn't.

The test: Does the direct connection create better knowledge transfer than your translation, or do you discover why the hub-and-spoke model exists?

CHAPTER 7

Cross-Functional Fluency

Speaking Every Department's Language

Aligned functions multiply, misaligned ones divide.
The single biggest problem in communication
is the illusion that it has taken place.

—GEORGE BERNARD SHAW

Often, the bigger problem in organizations is that communication happens in functional languages that other departments can't understand.

Maya's words wouldn't leave Alex alone: *You're not coordinating. You're translating. And we're not learning the language.*

Translation creates dependency. Fluency creates capability.

The distinction was everything. But how do you teach an entire organization to speak each other's languages?

The Microsoft Lesson: Systems over Translation

When Satya Nadella became CEO of Microsoft in 2014, he inherited a culture where proving others wrong was literally rewarded. I witnessed this firsthand. During my years managing Microsoft as an account, my main contact proudly displayed dollar bills taped to his whiteboard—trophies earned every time he proved someone else wrong. This systematic reinforcement of individual superiority over collaboration was limiting Microsoft's potential.

Nadella's insight: The problem wasn't that people couldn't communicate—it was that they had no reason to understand each other. Instead of hiring more translators or mandating collaboration, he redesigned the system. He changed performance metrics from individual brilliance to team impact, built cross-functional glossaries explaining what terms meant to each function, designed rotation programs where engineers spent time with sales and vice versa, and aligned bonuses to cross-functional collaboration scores.

Within three years, teams that had operated as warring kingdoms began speaking each other's languages fluently enough to solve problems no single function could address. The development of Microsoft Teams would have been impossible under the old translation-dependent model.

The results were measurable: Microsoft's market capitalization grew from roughly $300 billion when Nadella took over to over $3 trillion a decade later[1]—a tenfold increase, while the broader market grew less than twofold.

Building the Bridges: From Translation Dependency to Cross-Functional Fluency

The next morning, Alex did something unusual. He declined a meeting request.

Marcus from sales had asked him to "help engineering understand the customer urgency" on a pending integration. Instead, Alex wrote: "Marcus—I'm going to try something different. Can you and Chen meet directly? But before you do: Marcus, explain to Chen what the customer is actually trying to accomplish (not what they asked for). Chen, explain to Marcus what makes this technically complex (not why we can't do it). I'll join for the last fifteen minutes if you get stuck."

Marcus replied immediately: "Honestly, we'll probably need you the whole time."

Alex's fingers hovered over the keyboard. Every instinct wanted to agree. Instead, he typed: "Try it without me first. Worst case, we learn what makes direct coordination difficult."

Two hours later, Alex got a surprise Slack message from Chen: "That actually worked. Marcus explained that the customer doesn't need custom integration—they need faster onboarding for their specific data format. That's a totally different technical problem. We can solve it with a config template, not custom code. Three weeks instead of six months."

Alex's shoulders dropped. The relief was physical—not the dopamine hit of being the answer, but something deeper. They'd coordinated directly. They'd solved a problem better than he would have because they'd talked to each other in ways his translation would have filtered.

It was the bridge-building breakthrough. Not faster translation, but actual fluency.

Over the next two weeks, Alex ran an experiment. Every coordination request, he asked himself: *Is this a vocabulary gap, a context gap, or a metric gap?*

Then instead of translating, he built a bridge:

- **For vocabulary gaps:** He created a cross-functional translation cheat sheet—a simple document explaining what common terms meant to each function:

  Sales says "speed" ➔ engineering hears "reckless."

  Bridge: "Fast iteration on customer feedback" = sales priority, "Stable, scalable systems" = engineering priority. Both valid. The question: How do we learn quickly without breaking things?

- **For context gaps:** He set up "day in the life" swaps—thirty-minute sessions where functions explained their constraints and priorities to each other.
- **For metric gaps:** He designed shared success metrics that required functions to succeed together. "Customer value delivered per dollar invested" required sales to close profitable deals, engineering to build efficiently, and finance to allocate resources wisely.

The Architecture That Works Without You

Six months later, Alex walked past a conference room and stopped mid-stride.

Marcus from sales and Chen from engineering were at the whiteboard together—no Alex, no agenda he'd set, just two people problem-solving directly.

"So if we build it modular here," Chen said, while sketching, "you can promise enterprise customers this level of customization without us rebuilding everything each time?"

"Exactly." Marcus nodded. "And I can explain to customers why this approach gives them *more* flexibility long term, not less."

Alex noticed the translation cheat sheet taped to the wall behind them. Both were using the shared vocabulary framework—not perfectly, but fluently enough to coordinate without translation.

They didn't need him. They'd learned each other's language.

Alex paused at the door, a hint of a smile on his face. The architecture was working.

He kept walking.

Three weeks later, Alex reviewed the data:

- Translation meetings: Down 67 percent
- Cross-functional decisions: Three times faster
- His calendar: Eighteen hours per week freed up
- Team feedback: "We finally understand how the company works."

But the real test came when Alex took his first real vacation in four years—two weeks completely offline in Japan.

He returned to find an email thread with the subject: Major Enterprise Integration—Shipped While You Were Gone.

Marcus had written: "Alex—hope Japan was amazing. Remember that Fortune 500 integration that seemed impossible? Sales, engineering, product, and finance worked it out directly using the interface contracts you taught us. Shipped yesterday. Customer thrilled. Zero escalations.

We used the frameworks you designed but adapted them in ways you wouldn't have thought of."

Alex read the implementation details. The solution was better than what he would have built—because it incorporated constraints and opportunities he wouldn't have seen on his own.

"It worked *without* me," Alex whispered. Not despite his absence, but because of the systems he'd built.

The Identity Crisis of the Universal Translator

For Alex, the hardest part wasn't technical—it was psychological. When teams started coordinating without his translation, the relief was real—but so was the existential panic.

What am I if I'm not the universal translator?

His brain offered compelling answers: Less valuable. Less needed. Less relevant.

But those fears proved exactly backward. As translation demands decreased, Alex discovered he could finally do the work only he could do: designing the systems that enabled organizational intelligence no individual could provide.

The identity shift: From being the answer to building the architecture that generates answers.

This transformation triggers resistance in most leaders because our brains equate "needed for translation" with "valuable." The neurological reward of solving communication problems creates dependency—on you, certainly, but also in you.

The breakthrough comes when you realize this: A leader who can translate between any two functions is valuable. A leader who builds systems in which functions translate fluently without intervention creates something more valuable than themselves.

Your Translation Dependency Reality Check

Cross-functional fluency isn't about attitude—it's about information-flow patterns. Five questions diagnose your current approach.

QUICK TRANSLATION DEPENDENCY CHECK

1. When I'm out for a day, do cross-functional decisions wait for my return?
   - ✓ Yes = Controller pattern
   - ✓ Sometimes = Builder pattern
   - ✓ Rarely = Architect pattern
2. What percentage of my meeting time is spent translating between departments?
   - ✓ 60-plus percent = Controller bottleneck
   - ✓ 30–50 percent = Builder transition
   - ✓ Less than 20 percent = Architect systems working
3. Have I explained the same cross-functional concept to the same people three or more times?
   - ✓ Yes = Translation dependency exists
   - ✓ Occasionally = Bridge building in progress
   - ✓ No = Fluency achieved
4. When I connect two departments, what happens next time they need to coordinate?
   - ✓ Come to me again = Controller dependency
   - ✓ Sometimes bypass me = Builder progress
   - ✓ Coordinate directly = Architect fluency
5. If I list my top five time-consuming activities, how many involve cross-functional translation?
   - ✓ Three to five activities = Controller mode dominates
   - ✓ One to two activities = Builder mode developing
   - ✓ Zero activities = Architect systems functioning

Scoring

- ⦿ Mostly Controller patterns: You're the translation bottleneck (60-plus percent of coordination flows through you).

- Mostly Builder patterns: You're building bridges (functions coordinate directly 30 to 50 percent of the time).
- Mostly Architect patterns: You've built fluency (functions coordinate directly 70 percent or more of the time).

Design Moves: From Fluency to Collective Intelligence

Three lightweight artifacts turn cross-functional fluency into better-than-individual thinking:

- **Interface contracts:** Use for any shared decision, document inputs, required evidence, acceptable ranges, and timing between functions. This prevents rework and eliminates hidden assumptions.
- **Decision pre-briefs:** Keep to one page, always the same sections: what we're solving, what matters to each function, trade-offs we accept, downstream effects we anticipate. Pre-briefs force each function to think in the other's terms before the meeting.
- **Perspective ledger:** List who must be consulted versus merely informed, and the specific signal each brings. This keeps the right minds in the loop without slowing the system.

The Immediate Move

Look at your map. Pick the *one* most frequent translation pattern (the thickest arrow through you).

This week, instead of translating again, create the bridge:

- **If it's a vocabulary gap:** Document the translation once; give it to both functions.
- **If it's a context gap:** Set up a thirty-minute "day in the life" swap between functions.
- **If it's a metrics gap:** Design one shared success metric both functions care about.

Track whether they coordinate directly next time without involving you.

For systematic fluency architecture—shared metrics, decision integration, knowledge flow systems—see the Cross-Functional Fluency Framework in appendix I (access the appendices at catalystgrowthadvisors.com/the-hero-trap/).

The Fluency Choice

Cross-functional fluency was working beautifully within ParagonCX. Sales, engineering, and legal collaborated directly on enterprise deals. Customer success contributed to product decisions. The internal translation bottlenecks had largely disappeared.

But Alex's internal success had revealed a larger challenge: Every organization operates within an ecosystem of stakeholders whose interests must align for sustainable success. External partners, customers, investors, and regulators all had their own languages, priorities, and success metrics that didn't automatically align with ParagonCX's newly fluent internal systems.

The question wasn't whether to expand beyond internal fluency, but how to design systems that created stakeholder alignment automatically rather than requiring constant mediation.

The Signal Box

Cross-functional fluency isn't just about better coordination—it's about organizational multiplication. When functions understand each other well enough to collaborate naturally, problems get solved that no individual department could tackle alone.

Key insights from this chapter:

- Heroes translate between functions; Architects build systems where functions speak each other's languages fluently.

- Systems beat heroics because translation creates bottlenecks while fluency enables exponential coordination.
- The identity shift: from being the answer to building the architecture that generates answers.

Every gap you bridge personally is a gap your organization never learns to cross.

> **If you remember only one thing: Every time you translate between functions, you teach them they can't understand each other.**

Learning Prompt

Here's what I've observed: Most organizational friction comes from good people in different functions who literally can't understand each other's priorities and constraints.

Think about the last cross-functional conflict you mediated. What would have needed to be different for those teams to resolve it directly without your involvement?

This week, instead of translating between functions yourself, create one simple way for them to understand each other's language and constraints directly.

The experiment: Test whether building cross-functional fluency reduces coordination problems or reveals why central translation is sometimes necessary.

CHAPTER 8

Stakeholder Architecture

Designing Alignment at Every Level

Good stakeholder relationships are well-grounded.
Great ones defy gravity.

Alex noticed it first in his calendar. A dozen alignment meetings. A growing list of "quick calls" to smooth things over between investors and engineering, between enterprise clients and product.

He'd seen this before—with internal teams. The translation trap. He was building it again, just with external stakeholders.

This time, he caught it early.

Internal fluency had solved coordination between departments. But ParagonCX didn't operate in isolation. Investors wanted growth. Enterprise clients wanted reliability. Engineering wanted excellence. Sales wanted speed. Each group had legitimate priorities that didn't automatically align—and Alex had been drifting back toward his old role: the human middleware who made conflicting interests work through sheer effort.

That wasn't architecture. That was heroics wearing a different costume.

He needed a way to align the entire ecosystem—people he couldn't train, control, or even always meet—without personally refereeing every conflict.

Stakeholder architecture is the natural evolution of cross-functional fluency—scaling systematic alignment beyond internal teams to include everyone whose success affects your organization's ability to thrive.

Where cross-functional fluency solves the translation problem between departments, stakeholder architecture solves the alignment problem between all the groups that influence your success: customers, investors, partners, regulators, suppliers, and internal teams working together as an integrated ecosystem.

At ParagonCX, Alex realized that mastering internal fluency had prepared him for this challenge, but the scale and complexity were different. Internal teams could learn to speak each other's languages. External stakeholders couldn't be trained—they had to be aligned through systematic design that honored their existing priorities while creating shared value.

The architecture Alex needed would align enterprise customers seeking reliability, investors demanding growth, engineering teams pursuing excellence, and sales teams driving revenue—not through heroic mediation, but through systems that made stakeholder success mutually reinforcing.

Why Some Stakeholders Resist Systems Thinking

Alan Mulally's stakeholder-alignment success at Ford wasn't just about better process design. It was about understanding why intelligent, well-intentioned stakeholders naturally resist architectural thinking, even when it would benefit them.

The resistance wasn't logical. Ford's union leaders understood that systematic approaches would save jobs. The dealers knew that integrated systems would serve customers better. The suppliers recognized that architectural thinking would create more stable partnerships long term.

Yet each group initially resisted Mulally's "One Ford" systematic approach—not because they disagreed with the logic, but because systems thinking violated their fundamental values about how work should be organized and decisions should be made.

Most leaders assume stakeholder resistance is about the logic of the decision, the data being used, or the goals being set. In practice, that's rarely the case. What feels like conflict is usually a clash of underlying values—quality versus speed, autonomy versus control, innovation versus reliability. If you don't surface those values, you end up debating the wrong things and wondering why agreement never sticks.

Understanding Values-Based Resistance

As we explored in chapter 4 with Alex's membership design challenge, research by evolutionary psychologist Jonathan Haidt reveals that people resist change not primarily for rational reasons, but because change violates their moral foundations—their deeply held beliefs about what feels "right" or "wrong" in how organizations should operate.[1]

Alex discovered this firsthand at ParagonCX. When engineering pushed for reliability while sales pressed for speed, it looked like a fight over priorities. In reality, it was a clash of values—quality versus growth. Once Alex reframed the tension that way, he stopped trying to "win" the argument and started designing systems that honored both values. The result wasn't compromise; it was alignment that gave both groups more of what they needed.

Different stakeholder groups resist for different values-based reasons:

- **Authority/respect stakeholders** (senior engineers, subject matter experts) value expertise recognition. Response: Ask them to help design the system based on their experience.
- **Loyalty/betrayal stakeholders** (team leads, middle management) value team solidarity. Response: Frame systems as protecting collective success.
- **Care/harm stakeholders** (HR, customer success) value individual well-being. Response: Show how systems reduce long-term stress.
- **Fairness/cheating stakeholders** (finance, operations) value consistent rules. Response: Emphasize transparent processes that apply equally.
- **Liberty/oppression stakeholders** (sales, creative teams) value autonomy and flexibility. Response: Show how systems create more freedom by handling routine decisions.

The architecture implication: Instead of asking "How do I convince stakeholders that systems thinking is better?" ask "How do I design systems that feel right to each stakeholder group's core values?"

The goal isn't to change what stakeholders value—it's to design architectural approaches that advance systematic thinking while respecting the values that make stakeholders effective.

• • • •

At Ford, Mulally's breakthrough came when he stopped treating resistance as an education problem and started treating it as a stakeholder alignment challenge. Instead of explaining why systems thinking was better, he applied his "Working Together" Leadership and Management System, which included all stakeholders in the solution.[2]

Mulally attributed his success to including all stakeholders in the solution, explaining that his approach at both Boeing and Ford involved suppliers, customers, dealers, bankers, and investors—not just shareholders.

Rather than thinking of other individuals and organizations as competitors, Mulally employs a "win-win" mindset and approach in relationships. It helped him forge an agreement with the United Auto Workers union to make certain changes necessary for Ford to make a profit in return for bringing production back to the United States.

Alex's Stakeholder Architecture Discovery

Three years into Alex's Architect transformation, with ParagonCX now at 180 employees, they faced a stakeholder challenge that tested the limits of individual mediation.

The situation was complex: ParagonCX was approaching Series C funding while simultaneously expanding into enterprise markets and scaling their engineering team. Each stakeholder group had legitimate but seemingly conflicting needs. Investors wanted predictable revenue growth and a clear path to profitability. Enterprise customers needed customized solutions and dedicated support. The engineering team required time for technical debt reduction and architecture improvements. Sales needed product features that enabled faster deal closure. Customer success wanted product reliability and easier implementation processes.

Alex's initial response was the traditional approach—managing stakeholder conflicts through individual negotiation. He spent 60 percent of his time in stakeholder meetings, becoming the bottleneck for alignment. Strategic execution slowed as stakeholder management consumed increasing bandwidth, and conflicts recurred because underlying interests weren't systematically addressed.

But Alex was about to discover that stakeholder architecture follows a predictable progression, which he could use to design systems that move through each level systematically.

Level 1: The Mapping Breakthrough

Alex's first insight came when he stopped assuming he understood what stakeholders wanted and mapped their real needs. He discovered that most stakeholder conflicts came from unclear or incompatible expectations that had never been explicitly coordinated.

Take the enterprise customer situation. On the surface, it seemed like customers wanted maximum customization, which conflicted with engineering's need for standardized, excellent technology. But when Alex dug deeper into underlying interests rather than stated positions, he found something different: Enterprise customers wanted reliability and rapid value realization more than customization. Engineering teams wanted to build excellent technology that customers loved. Investors wanted predictable growth from satisfied customers.

The breakthrough was realizing that all three interests could be served by building modular, high-quality solutions that delivered fast customer value.

This was Alex's introduction to the difference between what stakeholders say they want (positions) and why they want it (underlying interests and concerns). Surface-level stakeholder conflicts often mask compatible underlying interests.

Level 2: Designing Mutual Value

Once Alex understood real stakeholder interests, he could design systems where serving one stakeholder's interests also served others'. The insight was simple but powerful: Sustainable alignment happens when each stakeholder's success reinforces rather than competes with others' success.

Alex applied this at ParagonCX by creating what he called "shared success metrics." Instead of separate goals for each group, he designed measures that required multiple stakeholders to succeed together. Customer success metrics became tied to engineering team recognition and advancement. Sales compensation aligned with customer long-term value, not just deal size. Engineering innovation time correlated with customer impact and business growth. Investor returns connected to sustainable customer value creation.

The transformation was dramatic. Each stakeholder's success started making others more successful. More satisfied customers led to better engineering recognition, which led to better product quality, resulting in happier customers and investors.

Level 3: Communication That Creates Alignment

But Alex discovered that good intentions and aligned interests weren't enough. Stakeholders needed systematic ways to stay aligned as situations changed. This led to his third major insight: Stakeholder communication could either create alignment or cause confusion, depending on how it was designed.

Alex built what he called "communication architecture" at ParagonCX. Monthly stakeholder updates shared the same strategic context with investors, customers, and internal teams—no more separate stories for different audiences. A transparent metrics dashboard showed customer success, engineering quality, and business growth, making everyone's contribution visible. Quarterly stakeholder input sessions meant feedback influenced strategic decisions rather than just being collected.

The result was that stakeholders started understanding how their success connected to others' success, and they began making decisions that naturally supported the whole system.

Level 4: Self-Reinforcing Systems

Alex's final discovery was the most powerful: The best stakeholder architecture creates feedback loops where aligned behavior becomes easier and more rewarding than misaligned behavior. This meant designing systems that would strengthen alignment automatically over time without constant management.

At ParagonCX, this showed up as early warning metrics that predicted stakeholder misalignment before it became a crisis. A systematic process distinguished between genuine interest conflicts and communication failures. Clear escalation procedures addressed conflicts through interest alignment rather than authority override.

But the real breakthrough came when a major enterprise customer requested significant customization. The sales, engineering, and customer success teams collaborated directly to develop a modular solution that served the customer's underlying needs while strengthening the platform for all stakeholders, without requiring Alex's mediation.

Alex realized he had built something that worked without him. The system had become what Nassim Taleb calls *antifragile*—challenges and stress made the stakeholder relationships stronger rather than weaker.

The Results

After twelve months of building this stakeholder architecture, the transformation was measurable. Stakeholder conflict resolution time decreased 70 percent as architecture prevented most conflicts. Strategic execution speed increased 60 percent as stakeholder alignment supported rather than constrained decisions. Customer satisfaction increased while engineering quality improved 40 percent. Investor confidence grew as predictable systems delivered consistent results.

Most importantly for Alex's Architect journey: His time allocation shifted from stakeholder mediation to strategic leadership and external opportunities. He had successfully designed systems that aligned stakeholders around shared value creation rather than requiring his constant intervention.

Your Stakeholder Architecture Reality Check

As Alex learned, most leaders can diagnose their current approach with a few simple questions.

Do stakeholders come to you to resolve their conflicts, or do they work things out directly? Are your stakeholder solutions typically win-win or zero-sum compromises? Do stakeholder relationships improve on their own, or do they require constant management?

If most answers point to personal mediation and constant management, you're where Alex started—in individual mediation mode. If you see progress toward automatic alignment, you're building stakeholder architecture.

The progression Alex discovered—from mapping to mutual value to communication systems to self-reinforcing alignment—provides a road map for any leader ready to move from stakeholder mediation to stakeholder architecture.

When your stakeholders routinely align themselves with shared objectives without requiring your mediation, you've built stakeholder architecture.

The difference between mediating and designing is the difference between spending energy and investing it. One exhausts you; the other compounds without you.

But Alex was about to discover that building stakeholder architecture and surviving its ultimate test were two very different challenges.

> *For systematic stakeholder architecture tools, see appendix I: the Stakeholder Architecture Framework for designing systems that align interests automatically, the Decision Architecture Matrix for clarifying decision rights across stakeholders, and the Resistance Cheat Sheet for anticipating values-based resistance to change (access the appendices at* catalystgrowthadvisors.com/the-hero-trap/*).*

The Signal Box

Stakeholder architecture transforms leadership from constant mediation to systematic alignment that strengthens over time.

Key insights from this chapter:

- Heroes mediate stakeholder conflicts; Architects design stakeholder alignment.
- Systems beat heroics because mediation creates dependency while architecture creates momentum.
- Your brain is wired for individual relationship management, but organizational success requires systematic alignment.
- There are four architecture levels: mapping, interest analysis, value creation design, and self-reinforcing systems.
- The goal isn't eliminating stakeholder conflicts. It's designing systems where stakeholder success reinforces rather than competes.
- Sustainable alignment happens when underlying interests are addressed rather than surface positions managed.

> **If you remember only one thing: When the same conflict keeps returning, the problem isn't the people, it's the design.**

Learning Prompt

Every leader I know has experienced both aligned stakeholders (where everyone's interests naturally reinforce each other) and competing stakeholders (where satisfying one group frustrates another).

Think about your current stakeholder challenges. What would need to be true for their interests to align automatically rather than requiring your constant mediation?

This week, identify one stakeholder conflict that keeps recurring and design one systematic change that could align their interests rather than just managing the tension.

The insight: Sometimes stakeholder conflicts signal design problems in how value gets created and distributed, not just communication problems.

PART III

CALMER: FINDING PEACE IN COMPLEXITY AND UNCERTAINTY

THE FINAL DIMENSION OF ARCHITECTURAL leadership is the most counterintuitive: finding calm in complexity. This requires strategic patience over reactive speed, comfort with uncertainty over illusions of control, fulfillment through others' success over personal heroics, and building systems that work without you. When you master the "calmer" dimension, leadership becomes sustainable rather than exhausting.

- **WHERE YOU'VE BEEN:** You've built systems that work without you. Others are making decisions you used to make—sometimes better than you would have.
- **WHERE YOU'RE GOING:** From designing systems to trusting them. From proving the architecture works to letting it evolve beyond you.
- **CHAPTERS 9–12** help you develop strategic patience, lead through uncertainty, find fulfillment in others' success, and build systems that improve without you.
- **YOU'VE ARRIVED WHEN:** You return from vacation to find things didn't just survive—they got better.

CHAPTER 9

The Patience Paradox

Why Slower Decisions Create Faster Results

Rushed foundations create years of cracks.

For Alex, the cracks were showing. The first warning came during the Tuesday all-hands. Alex was mid-sentence—something about Q3 priorities and the enterprise push—when his vision went gray at the edges. The room tilted slightly. His hand found the podium, and he heard his own voice continue from somewhere far away.

"—and that's why we're prioritizing the Meridian segment for—"

Someone said his name. Maybe twice. Then he was sitting in a chair he didn't remember reaching, and Sarah was pressing a water bottle into his hand while sixty employees tried not to stare.

"When did you last eat?" she asked quietly.

Alex tried to remember. Breakfast? No—that had been coffee. Dinner last night? He'd meant to, but the board prep had run late, and then there was the Slack thread about the deployment issue, and by the time he looked up, it was midnight—and eating felt like more effort than sleeping.

"I'm fine," he said. "Just stood up too fast."

Sarah didn't argue. She just looked at him the way Emma had started looking at him—like she was watching something break in slow motion and couldn't figure out how to stop it.

The all-hands resumed. Alex got through it. But that night, for the first time, he searched "signs of burnout" on his phone with the bedroom door closed, scrolling past articles that described his last six months with uncomfortable precision.

Chronic exhaustion that sleep doesn't fix. Cynicism about work that used to energize you. Physical symptoms your doctor can't explain.

He closed the browser and stared at the ceiling.

The cracks weren't just showing in the company anymore. They were showing in him.

ParagonCX was scaling fast, but the pace was starting to feel like speed for speed's sake—features shipping half-finished, decisions made to quiet anxiety instead of build strength. Every "fast" win created two new problems to fix later.

He could feel the old pattern returning: relief now, regret later. The same instinct that once built the company was now making it brittle.

He didn't need another framework. He needed a forcing function that would make excellence unavoidable—even when the board demanded velocity.

The First Principles Breakthrough: Finding Your Forcing Function

What's the *one* thing you could focus on that would force excellence in every system simultaneously?

Not the outcome you want to achieve. Not the quarterly target you need to hit. But the single "ungameable" metric that would make operational excellence inevitable rather than optional.

Most leaders never find it. They chase outcomes directly and wonder why improvements don't last.

Architects work differently. They identify the foundational requirement that makes desired outcomes inevitable. They design forcing functions that cannot be gamed and demand systematic excellence.

The pattern appears across decades and industries. In 1987, a CEO chose worker safety when Wall Street demanded profits. In 2014, a CEO chose customer health when investors demanded growth. Today, a founder chose environmental responsibility when conventional wisdom demanded maximum growth. In each case, the counterintuitive focus created compound results that direct optimization never could.

> **The principle is timeless. The results are measurable. And the strategic patience required still feels wrong to most leaders.**

O'Neill's Master Class in Systems Leverage

When Paul O'Neill became CEO of Alcoa in 1987, Wall Street expected the usual turnaround playbook: cut costs, slash workforce, boost quarterly earnings. The aluminum giant was struggling with safety issues, inconsistent quality, and stagnant profits. Investors wanted immediate financial results.

Instead, O'Neill made an announcement that stunned shareholders: "I want to talk to you about worker safety. Every year in America, 200,000 people go to an emergency room because of injuries suffered in the workplace. I intend to make Alcoa the safest company in America. I intend to go for zero injuries."

The room went silent. One investor stood up and walked out during the presentation. Others questioned whether O'Neill understood his job was to increase profits, not coddle workers.

The investors saw a distraction. O'Neill saw a lever.

The First Principles Discovery

While his critics saw a CEO who didn't understand business priorities, O'Neill was conducting advanced first principles thinking. He had worked backward from a fundamental question:

> **What would force this company to achieve operational excellence in every system simultaneously?**

Most leaders would have targeted profitability directly—the conventional approach. But O'Neill recognized that profitability was an *outcome*, not a *cause*. He needed to identify the *one foundational requirement* that would make operational excellence inevitable rather than optional.

His breakthrough insight: Safety was the perfect forcing function.

Why Safety Was the Ultimate Leverage Point

O'Neill understood something his critics missed: You cannot achieve zero injuries through shortcuts, politics, or quick fixes. Safety demands excellence in every supporting system:

- **Perfect communication systems:** Every injury required immediate investigation and company-wide communication. This forced transparency, rapid information flow, and systematic problem-solving across all departments.
- **Rigorous process analysis:** Preventing accidents required understanding exactly how work gets done, not how it was supposed to get done. This demanded process documentation, continuous improvement, and root cause analysis.
- **Employee engagement:** Frontline workers had to actively participate in identifying hazards and suggesting improvements. This required trust, psychological safety, and genuine two-way communication.
- **Cross-functional coordination:** Safety touches every department—engineering, operations, procurement, training, maintenance. Improving it required breaking down silos and optimizing whole systems, not individual parts.
- **Systematic thinking:** Preventing accidents required understanding interconnections, cascade effects, and how changes in one area rippled through entire operations.

> **This is first principles thinking in action: O'Neill identified *the one* metric that could not be gamed and would force excellence in every other capability the company needed.**

The Cascade Effect Architecture

The genius wasn't patience about safety versus impatience about profits. The genius was recognizing the *cascade architecture*—how focusing on the right foundational element would automatically improve everything else:

- **Second-order effects:** Better communication systems improved coordination, quality, and innovation.
- **Third-order effects:** Employee engagement increased productivity, reduced turnover, and generated continuous improvement ideas.
- **Fourth-order effects:** Process excellence reduced waste, improved quality, and accelerated production.
- **Fifth-order effects:** Cross-functional coordination enabled faster innovation, better customer service, and more efficient resource allocation.

The results proved the theory: Workplace injuries dropped twentyfold, productivity soared, and profits increased fivefold during O'Neill's tenure.[1] Alcoa's stock price grew over 200 percent while he systematically pursued what seemed like the "slowest" possible approach to business improvement.

"The One Thing" Principle Applied to Organizations

Gary Keller's concept "the One Thing" asks, "What's the ONE thing you can do such that by doing it everything else will be easier or unnecessary?"[2]

O'Neill answered this question at the organizational level. While competitors were trying to improve multiple metrics simultaneously, he identified the single focus that would force improvement in every metric that mattered.

Most business leaders focus on outcomes (profitability, growth, market share) and work forward through tactics. O'Neill focused on the foundational system requirement (operational excellence) and worked backward to identify the forcing function (safety) that would make excellence inevitable.

This is the difference between heroic leadership and architectural leadership:

- **Heroes optimize directly for desired outcomes**, often creating superficial improvements that don't last.
- **Architects identify the system requirements that make desired outcomes inevitable**, creating compound improvements that accelerate over time.

Your forcing function becomes the backbone of your architecture. The single focus that makes everything else easier or unnecessary.

The Strategic Pattern: Find Your "Safety" Metric

O'Neill's transformation demonstrates a replicable pattern for organizational change:

1. **Start with first principles:** What fundamental capabilities does your organization need to excel at everything else?
2. **Identify the forcing function:** What single metric or focus would *demand* excellence in all supporting systems?
3. **Choose something that cannot be gamed:** The metric must require genuine systematic improvement, not superficial optimization.
4. **Design for cascade effects:** Understand how improvements in this area will automatically strengthen other capabilities.
5. **Accept short-term misunderstanding:** True leverage points often seem "slow" or "indirect" to people focused on immediate outcomes.

This is the patience paradox—the Architect's understanding that strategic patience focused on the right leverage point creates operational speed across all systems.

The Forcing Function Test

How do you know you've found a true forcing function and not just another goal? Apply three tests:

- **It cannot be gamed:** If you can improve the metric through manipulation, politics, or superficial changes, it's not a forcing function. Real improvement must be the only path forward.
- **It can't be solved in a silo:** A true forcing function demands excellence across departments, not just in one silo. If only one team needs to change, you've found a project, not a forcing function.
- **It feels indirect:** If it seems like the obvious path to your goals, it's probably just a goal restated. True forcing functions make stakeholders uncomfortable precisely because they don't target outcomes directly.

O'Neill's safety focus passed all three tests. So did CVS CEO Larry Merlo's decision to stop selling tobacco. So did Patagonia founder Yvon Chouinard's environmental stand. In each case, the "indirect" path created results that direct optimization never could.

> *The Forcing Function Discovery Tool in the Tool Kit (appendix I) walks you through identifying your organization's forcing function—including how to map cascade effects and anticipate stakeholder resistance (access the appendices at* catalystgrowthadvisors.com/the-hero-trap/*).*

The Pattern Holds: Modern Forcing Functions

O'Neill's 1987 insight wasn't a one-time phenomenon. The forcing function pattern continues to create breakthrough results when leaders have the patience to apply it.

CVS Health: When Customer Health Forced Retail Excellence (2014)

In 2014, CVS CEO Larry Merlo faced his own moment of counterintuitive choice. Wall Street wanted growth. The board expected retail expansion. But Merlo announced CVS would stop selling tobacco products—eliminating $2 billion in annual revenue.

The reaction was predictable. Investors questioned the decision. The stock took a hit. Competitors celebrated gaining market share.

Analysts saw $2 billion in lost revenue. Merlo saw the barrier blocking a future that only removal would reveal.

Just like safety at Alcoa, customer health became CVS's ungameable forcing function:

- **It forced strategic coherence:** A pharmacy claiming to support health couldn't sell products that caused disease. The contradiction required resolution.
- **It forced operational excellence:** Transitioning from retail to healthcare demanded new capabilities—clinical services, care coordination, outcome measurement.
- **It forced stakeholder alignment:** Health outcomes unified pharmacy operations, insurance partnerships, and retail strategy under one compelling purpose.
- **It forced competitive differentiation:** Choosing health over tobacco revenue created a market position no competitor could easily replicate.

The patient decision created compound returns: CVS transformed from a retailer to a healthcare company, completed the $69 billion Aetna acquisition, and saw its stock price triple by 2024. The "costly" choice became the foundation for a sustainable competitive advantage.

Patagonia: When Environmental Responsibility Forced Business Excellence (Ongoing)

Patagonia founder Yvon Chouinard chose environmental responsibility as his forcing function.

The industry saw noise as the cost of competition. Chouinard saw the signal that would cut through—and attract everyone it had been ignoring.

Like safety at Alcoa and health at CVS, environmental responsibility couldn't be gamed:

- **It forced product excellence:** Durability and repairability were prioritized over planned obsolescence.
- **It forced supply chain transparency:** Knowing the environmental impact meant knowing every supplier.
- **It forced business model innovation:** "Don't Buy This Jacket" and a used-gear marketplace created advantages that competitors couldn't copy without abandoning their growth models.
- **It forced talent alignment:** People who wanted their work to mean something found a place that meant it.

Patagonia became one of the most valuable private companies in the apparel industry. Then Chouinard gave it away, transferring ownership to environmental preservation. The signal had attracted exactly the outcome he'd been building toward all along.

The Common Pattern

Across decades and industries, the forcing function principle remains consistent:

- **Choose something ungameable:** Injuries, health, and environmental impact are metrics that require real change, not superficial optimization.
- **Accept short-term costs:** Lost revenue, investor skepticism, competitive vulnerability are top candidates.
- **Force systematic excellence:** The metric demands improvement in every supporting system.
- **Create compound advantages:** Better systems generate sustainable competitive differentiation.

What O'Neill proved in 1987, CVS validated in 2014, and Patagonia demonstrates on an ongoing basis: **Strategic patience focused**

on the right forcing function creates operational speed across all systems.

This is the patience paradox that still escapes most leaders today.

But understanding the pattern intellectually doesn't make it easier to apply. O'Neill's transformation demonstrates the power of strategic patience, but it also raises a crucial question: If slower decisions create faster results, why do most leaders remain addicted to decision speed? The answer lies in how our brains are wired to resist the very patience that creates breakthrough performance.

BEHAVIORAL SCIENCE BOX
Why Your Brain Craves Decision Speed

The same neural wiring that made you a decisive operator now works against the strategic patience your role demands. Modern neuroscience reveals why leaders become addicted to fast decisions: Your brain interprets open decisions as threats requiring immediate resolution.

The Speed Addiction Circuit

- **Anxiety reduction:** Making decisions quickly provides immediate neurological relief.
- **Control restoration:** Fast action creates the illusion of control over uncertain outcomes.
- **Status validation:** Quick decisions make you appear competent and decisive.
- **Dopamine release:** Completion provides immediate neurological rewards.

The Strategic Patience Resistance

- **Uncertainty tolerance:** Patient decision-making requires sitting with discomfort.

- **Social pressure:** Stakeholders often reward speed over quality, threatening your sense of relatedness and fairness.
- **Opportunity cost anxiety:** Waiting feels like missing opportunities, reducing your sense of autonomy.
- **Analysis paralysis fear:** This is the concern that more thinking leads to overthinking.

THE PREFRONTAL CORTEX ADVANTAGE

Research shows that strategic patience activates the prefrontal cortex—the brain region responsible for complex reasoning, future planning, and inhibitory control. These are precisely the capabilities required for architectural leadership.

When Paul O'Neill chose safety as Alcoa's strategic focus, his leadership team initially resisted the "slow" approach. The neurological reality: Their brains craved the immediate satisfaction of traditional profit-focused decisions. But O'Neill's strategic patience created compound returns that no quick decision could match—workplace injuries dropped by 95 percent, while market capitalization increased fivefold.

Your brain will resist strategic patience until you experience compound returns from thoughtful decision-making.

Use the CBA lens here: Notice when you're reacting as a Controller, coaching as a Builder, or designing patience into the system as an Architect.

THIS WEEK: THE TWENTY-FOUR-HOUR PATIENCE EXPERIMENT

Pick one decision you'd normally make immediately and add twenty-four hours to your timeline.

Not because slow is always better—but to notice what your brain does with that extra time. Does the anxiety decrease or increase? Does clarity emerge or does analysis paralysis set in? Does the decision improve or does your first instinct prove right?

The goal isn't to always slow down. It's to understand when patience serves you and when it doesn't.

PARAGONCX'S SPEED-TO-PATIENCE EVOLUTION

Three years into Alex's Architect transformation, ParagonCX faced a foundational decision that tested his patience paradox understanding.

The decision: Whether to build their own AI infrastructure or partner with a major cloud provider for their machine-learning capabilities.

When the board pressed for immediate answers, Alex felt his old Controller identity clawing back to the surface, promising the relief of quick action.

The Hero Approach (Alex's Old Instincts)

- Research for two to three days maximum.
- Make the decision based on immediate technical and cost factors.
- Move quickly to avoid competitive disadvantage.
- Adjust course if problems emerged.

The Architect Approach (Alex's Evolved Approach)

- Invest six weeks in comprehensive analysis.
- Consider technical, strategic, financial, and organizational implications.
- Involve engineering, finance, sales, and customer success perspectives.
- Model scenarios two to three years into the future.

The Patience Investment

- **Weeks one and two:** Technical feasibility analysis for both options

- **Weeks three and four:** Financial modeling, including hidden costs and scaling implications
- **Weeks five and six:** Strategic impact assessment, including competitive positioning and future optionality

The Patient Decision Process

- **Scenario planning:** Alex's team modeled three growth scenarios (conservative, expected, aggressive) and analyzed how each infrastructure choice would perform under different conditions.
- **Stakeholder integration:** Instead of making the decision, Alex designed a process where engineering, finance, sales, and customer success each contributed their expertise to the decision architecture.
- **Future optionality analysis:** Rather than optimizing for immediate needs, the team analyzed which choice would create more strategic options as the company scaled.
- **The breakthrough insight:** The patient analysis revealed that the immediate cost savings of cloud partnership would be offset by reduced strategic optionality and potential vendor lock-in as they scaled. The "expensive" decision to build internal infrastructure would accelerate long-term growth and competitive differentiation.

Results After Eighteen Months

- Internal AI infrastructure became a competitive advantage that cloud partners couldn't match.
- Development speed increased 40 percent because teams could optimize infrastructure for their specific needs.
- Customer satisfaction improved 35 percent due to better performance and customization capabilities.

- The patient decision created capabilities that enabled product innovations competitors couldn't replicate.

Alex's reflection: "Six weeks of patient analysis saved us eighteen months of suboptimal execution. The decision that felt slow became the foundation for faster everything else."

Strategic patience had become Alex's competitive advantage.

The real test would come when market pressures forced him to choose between his carefully built long-term systems and short-term survival. When the stakes were highest and time was shortest, would he revert to hero mode—or would his architectural thinking hold under fire?

For comprehensive strategic patience tools, see appendix I: the Strategic Patience Assessment & Development System for diagnosing speed-bias patterns, the Time Horizon Audit for balancing immediate versus long-term focus, the Forcing Function Discovery Tool for identifying your organization's leverage point, and the Decision Architecture Matrix for matching decision velocity to decision type (access the appendices at catalystgrowthadvisors.com/the-hero-trap/*).*

The Signal Box

Strategic patience focused on the right forcing function creates operational speed across every system.

Key insights from this chapter:

- Most urgency is impatience wearing a disguise—your brain rewards speed because completion feels like control.
- Heroes optimize directly for outcomes; Architects identify the foundational requirement that makes desired outcomes inevitable.

- A true forcing function cannot be gamed, cannot be solved in a silo, and feels indirect—if it looks like the obvious path, it's probably just a restated goal.
- The pattern holds across decades: O'Neill's safety at Alcoa, Merlo's customer health at CVS, Chouinard's environmental responsibility at Patagonia.
- Six weeks of patient analysis can save eighteen months of suboptimal execution—the decision that feels slow becomes the foundation for faster everything else.

When the choice that looks costly becomes the foundation that makes every other system stronger, you've found your forcing function.

> **If you remember only one thing: Most urgency is impatience wearing a disguise.**

Learning Prompt

You've experienced both: decisions that got better because you took time, and decisions that got worse because you waited too long.

Think about that decision you're facing right now. What's driving the pressure to decide quickly—real urgency, or the discomfort of not knowing?

Try adding one day to your timeline and see what emerges. Not because slow is always better, but because you might discover whether the urgency is helping your thinking or hurting it.

The learning: Sometimes strategic patience reveals insights that save weeks of execution time. Sometimes it confirms your first instinct was right. Both discoveries are valuable.

CHAPTER 10

Comfortable with Chaos

Leading When You Don't Have All the Answers

Chaos favors the prepared mind.

Alex had always thought preparation meant certainty—clear plans, crisp answers, and no surprises. He was about to learn that real preparation meant something else entirely: being ready to lead when nothing went according to plan.

But first, he had to fail.

The week before the RevenueCorp crisis, everything came apart at once.

Meridian Technologies, their second-largest customer, announced they were "evaluating alternatives." Two engineers gave notice on the same day—both citing burnout. A critical security vulnerability required an emergency patch that delayed the product road map by three weeks. And the board called an unscheduled meeting to discuss "concerns about execution."

Alex lasted four days.

On day one, he told himself to trust the systems. On day two, he joined a few meetings "just to observe." By day three, he was running the incident response himself, reassigning engineers without consulting their managers, and sending emails at midnight that began with "I need you to . . ."

On day four, Maya found him in the conference room at 7 a.m., surrounded by sticky notes, rewriting the product road map she'd finalized two weeks earlier.

She didn't say anything. She just stood in the doorway.

"I know," Alex said, not looking up. "I know what this looks like."

"What does it look like?"

"Like I'm doing exactly what I said I'd stop doing."

"That's what it looks like to me too."

Alex put down his pen. His hands were shaking slightly—not from caffeine, though he'd had plenty, but from the specific exhaustion of trying to hold everything together by force of will.

"Meridian is going to leave," he said. "The board is asking questions I can't answer. I can't just . . ." He stopped. "I can't just *watch* it fall apart."

Maya walked to the whiteboard and erased one of his diagrams. "What did you tell me six months ago, when I wanted to override the traffic light system during the Nexfield situation?"

Alex remembered. "I said the system only works if we let it work."

"And what happened with Nexfield?"

"Sarah handled it. Better than I would have."

Maya sat down across from him. "Alex, I'm not going to pretend this week hasn't been hard. It has. But you've spent the last four days undoing three months of work. Not the crisis—*your response* to the crisis. People are confused about who has authority. Teams are waiting for your approval again because you've been inserting yourself everywhere. The trust we built is quieter now."

Quieter. The word stayed with him.

Alex looked at the sticky notes. At the road map he'd rewritten. At the calendar on his laptop showing twelve meetings he'd scheduled for himself.

"I thought . . ." He stopped. "I don't know what I thought."

"Transformation isn't a line," Maya said. "It's a spiral. You're going to hit old patterns under pressure. Every leader does. The question isn't whether you'll regress. It's whether you'll recognize it faster each time."

Alex sat with that for a long moment. He couldn't look at her.

"What do I do now?"

"Undo what you did. Go to Sarah and Marcus and tell them you overstepped. Give the road map back to me. Cancel the meetings you don't need to be in. And then—" Maya paused. "And then trust that we can handle this. Not because everything will be perfect, but because we've built something that's stronger than any one person's panic."

The next week was one of the hardest of Alex's career. Not because the crises got worse—they didn't. Sarah stabilized the engineering team. Marcus saved the Meridian relationship through a conversation Alex would have handled with less empathy and more urgency. The board meeting went better than expected because the team's response demonstrated exactly the organizational resilience the board wanted to see.

The hard part was watching it happen without being the hero.

Alex kept a note on his desk for months afterward: "The relapse wasn't the failure. Staying in relapse would have been."

That Saturday, he left his laptop at the office. It was the first small act of designing recovery into the system instead of waiting for collapse to force it.

The Real Test

Three years into his architectural transformation, Alex faced his ultimate test.

RevenueCorp, representing 40 percent of their monthly recurring revenue, had just terminated their contract. Their largest competitor was promising AI capabilities that didn't exist yet, and enterprise customers were believing them. Two key team members had given notice.

Twelve senior leaders stared at Alex, waiting for him to do what he'd always done: Present a plan, assign actions, rally the troops with confident certainty.

But Alex felt something different this time. Not panic—something closer to clarity.

"I don't know what we should do yet," he heard himself saying. "And that's exactly where we need to be right now."

The words surprised everyone, including Alex.

He walked to the whiteboard. Instead of drawing a solution, he wrote: "WHAT DON'T WE KNOW?"

"If I pretend to have answers I don't have, we'll make expensive mistakes based on outdated assumptions. But if we design our way through this uncertainty together, we might discover something our competitors can't imagine."

For the first time in months, Alex saw genuine engagement—not the polite attention they gave to his confident presentations, but active collaboration from people who felt safe to contribute their real thinking.

The conversation that followed was unlike any strategy session they'd had before. Instead of competing to be right, the team was collaborating to be accurate.

• • • •

Three weeks later, Alex sat watching a Slack thread between Marco, head of engineering, and Sarah. They were struggling with the Hendricks integration—the same type of problem Alex had solved dozens of times. He could see exactly where they were going wrong.

His fingers twitched toward the keyboard. *They're missing the obvious solution. I could explain it in ten minutes.*

He started typing: "Have you considered—"

Then stopped. Deleted the message. Closed Slack. Stood up because sitting there watching was too hard.

Twenty minutes later, he heard laughter from the engineering pod. Sarah was at the whiteboard explaining a solution Alex hadn't considered. Not his workaround—something better. Something that would scale.

He returned to his office and typed a note to himself: "They solved Hendricks without me. Solution was better than mine would have been. Didn't intervene. Didn't die."

The small, private record of a man learning to trust what he'd built.

Psychologists call this the *illusion of control*—the tendency to overestimate our ability to influence outcomes that are largely beyond our control. Alex had just discovered its twin: the *illusion of comprehension.*

Leaders believe they can manage the chaos because they believe they understand the systems generating it.

But as the complexity math in the introduction showed, that comprehension crossed into self-deception years ago. The systems inside your organization exceeded individual understanding long before you noticed. Accepting that you cannot hold it all—that no one can—isn't defeat. It's the prerequisite for designing systems that can.

The next Monday, Alex walked into his leadership team meeting and said something he'd never said before: "I made the migration call with maybe 40 percent of the information I needed. I didn't build systems that would have surfaced the rest. That's what we're fixing—starting now."

Three architectural principles emerged.

Three Core Navigation Principles

When Alex stopped trying to control uncertainty and started building systems to navigate it, three architectural principles emerged:

- **Information architecture**

  Distinguish what you know from what you don't know.

  Before: Alex projected confidence about recovery timelines to maintain team morale and investor confidence.

  After: Weekly "uncertainty updates" clearly distinguished:

  - What we know: Specific client concerns, competitive movements, verified market data
  - What we're learning: Active customer research, competitive analysis, product experiments
  - What we don't know: Future client behavior, competitive capabilities, regulatory outcomes
  - How we're adapting: Decision updates based on new information

  Result: Stakeholder trust increased because expectations were realistic and progress was measurable.

- **Option architecture**

  Create multiple approaches instead of betting on one path.

  Before: All major responses flowed through Alex for approval and coordination.

  After: Three parallel approaches with distributed authority:

  - Product team: Enhanced existing features based on customer feedback (autonomous development)
  - Sales team: New market segment exploration (weekly coordination check-ins)
  - Engineering team: Next-generation AI capabilities (monthly strategic review)

  Result: Response speed tripled while maintaining quality and avoiding resource conflicts.

- **Learning architecture**

  Build systems that adapt based on new information.

  Before: Setbacks felt like failures that required immediate fixes.

  After: Systematic learning integration:

  - Daily adaptation: Product features modified based on user feedback/behavior
  - Weekly sharing: Cross-team insight sessions revealing customer patterns
  - Monthly analysis: Systematic review of what approaches worked versus failed
  - Quarterly innovation: Permission to test unconventional solutions

  Result: ParagonCX emerged from the crisis with capabilities their competitors couldn't match.

The Foundation That Made It Work

Alex's uncertainty navigation succeeded because his team felt safe to say "I don't know" and "This isn't working." Without psychological safety, the entire systematic approach would have collapsed into false reporting and defensive decision-making.

The most effective uncertainty navigation comes from developing comfort with not knowing. When you're not spending mental energy fighting uncertainty or projecting false confidence, you can allocate that energy to pattern recognition, creative problem-solving, stakeholder communication, adaptive strategy development, and team coordination.

Without that safety, every other system collapses into false certainty.

The platform migration eventually shipped—eleven weeks late. But the version that launched wasn't Alex's design. It was Chen's architecture, pressure-tested by three teams who'd been given permission to challenge assumptions Alex would have defended a year earlier.

I didn't fail because I made the wrong call, Alex realized. *I failed because I was still the one making calls I shouldn't have been making alone.*

The two enterprise deals that had stalled? One came back. The other didn't. Alex stopped pretending that was a victory. It was a scar—and scars were how he remembered what not to do next time.

Alex would soon face that test himself. The next time he walked into a room full of people who wanted certainty, there wouldn't be time for analysis or frameworks—only the question of whether he truly trusted what he'd built.

The Signal Box

Real preparation isn't certainty about the answer–it's readiness to lead when nothing goes according to plan.

Key insights from this chapter:

- Transformation isn't a line; it's a spiral–the question isn't whether you'll regress under pressure, but whether you'll recognize it faster each time.

- The illusion of comprehension is the leader's twin to the illusion of control—you stopped understanding all the systems years ago.
- Three architectures replace heroic certainty: information (what we know versus don't know), option (parallel paths instead of one bet), and learning (systems that adapt as new information arrives).
- "I don't know" said honestly by the leader gives the team permission to stop pretending—and that's when real strategy begins.
- Psychological safety isn't a soft layer; without it, every other navigation system collapses into false reporting.

When your team feels safe to say "I don't know" before you do, you've built the foundation that makes every other architecture possible.

> **If you remember only one thing: Your team will only admit what they don't know after you go first.**

Learning Prompt

In your next leadership meeting, have everyone (including you) write down one "accepted truth"—one thing most people there assume is true but probably isn't.

Go around the room. Share them. Pick the most dangerous one to test this week.

The power isn't in being right about which truth is false. It's in normalizing the question: *What if we're wrong about this?*

Most teams discover they've been operating on assumptions no one dared to challenge—until the leader went first.

CHAPTER 11

Building a Room Smarter Than You

Parents who never let their kids fall raise adults who can't walk.

I measure my success not by our financial performance, but by how many people we've sent into the world more capable than when they arrived.

—BOB CHAPMAN, CEO, BARRY-WEHMILLER

In 1997, Bob Chapman walked into his first acquisition meeting as CEO of Barry-Wehmiller with a radical idea that made no sense to Wall Street: He wasn't going to fire anyone.[1]

The $20 million manufacturing company had just acquired a struggling facility, and every conventional business practice demanded immediate layoffs, management restructuring, and cost cutting. The acquired company's leadership team sat around the conference table, expecting pink slips and worrying about their futures.

Instead, Chapman asked a question that would define the next quarter-century of his leadership: "What if we could make this company successful by making its people more capable, rather than by making them gone?"

The room fell silent. This wasn't how acquisitions worked. You bought companies for their assets, eliminated redundancies, and imposed your systems from above. You didn't invest in developing people you'd inherited from a failing business.

But Chapman had a different theory about business success. He'd been studying companies that achieved sustainable growth, and he'd noticed something curious: The organizations that lasted weren't just good at making products—they were good at making people better at making products.

"I want to understand what you know about running this business," Chapman told the inherited leadership team. "Because you know things about these customers, these processes, and these markets that we don't. Instead of replacing you, what if we helped you become the best version of what you already are?"

Over the following months, Chapman implemented something unprecedented in the manufacturing world: He invested more in leadership development than in operational restructuring. Instead of installing Barry-Wehmiller's systems, he studied the acquired company's systems. Instead of imposing external managers, he developed internal capabilities. Instead of optimizing for immediate profits, he optimized for long-term people development.

The results confused competitors and delighted stakeholders. The acquisition succeeded beyond projections. The inherited leadership team not only stayed—they became some of Chapman's most effective developers of other leaders. Most remarkably, several of them eventually left to run other companies, taking their developed capabilities to create value elsewhere.

Chapman realized he'd discovered something more valuable than a successful acquisition strategy—he'd found the secret to scalable leadership itself.

Some leaders arrive at this insight through business logic: They calculate that organizational capability compounds while individual heroics plateau, and they design accordingly. Others arrive through human concern: They recognize that developing people is inherently valuable and discover it also builds better organizations.

These aren't competing philosophies. They're two doors into the same room.

Chapman walked through both simultaneously—investing in people because he believed they deserved development, and building a $2 billion enterprise because developed people create compounding value.

The leaders who try to optimize for one while neglecting the other eventually fail at both. The ones who recognize the integration build organizations that last.

The Development Breakthrough

What Chapman discovered wasn't just that developing people worked better than replacing them. He discovered that *his fulfillment as a leader* came not from making the best decisions but from building others who could make decisions better than he could.

This insight would drive Barry-Wehmiller's transformation from a regional manufacturer to a global enterprise worth over $2 billion—achieved through more than eighty acquisitions, with success rates that mystified industry analysts.

Chapman's approach violated every piece of conventional wisdom about acquisition integration:

- **Conventional wisdom:** Install your proven systems and management immediately.
- **Chapman's approach:** Study their systems first, then develop hybrid approaches that preserve local knowledge while adding Barry-Wehmiller capabilities.

- **Conventional wisdom:** Replace underperforming leadership with proven executives.
- **Chapman's approach:** Invest six months developing existing leadership, then evaluate performance after they'd had systematic development support.

- **Conventional wisdom:** Optimize for immediate synergies and cost reductions.
- **Chapman's approach:** Optimize for long-term capability development, accepting short-term costs for long-term competitive advantage.

The breakthrough wasn't in the techniques Chapman used. It was in understanding that his job wasn't to be the best leader in every acquired company. His job was to develop the best leaders for every acquired company.

What Chapman discovered went beyond acquisition strategy. It revealed why organizational capability systematically outperforms individual heroics.

Why this works: Traditional acquisition logic reflects old success patterns—hire proven executives, cut costs, impose control from above. But systems complexity explosion means no individual can master every domain of an acquired business. Chapman recognized that building organizational capability handles complexity better than individual heroics, even brilliant individual heroics. In a BANI environment where competitive advantage comes from adaptation speed, developing local expertise multiplies faster than replacing it.

This understanding became the foundation for Chapman's systematic approach to delegation. Not just at acquired companies, but throughout Barry-Wehmiller's operations.

This is the delegation breakthrough: The Architect's understanding that building the best problem solvers creates more business value than being the best problem solver, and often more fulfillment too—though that's a bonus, not the point.

Bob and Weave: Escaping the Hero Trap

The business case: Barry-Wehmiller grew from $20 million to over $2 billion through eighty-plus acquisitions with success rates that mystified analysts. Every problem Chapman solved personally was a problem the organization solved once. Every capability he built in others was a problem the organization solved forever—in situations he'd never see, with adaptations he'd never imagine. The compound returns on organizational capability dwarf the linear returns on individual excellence, no matter how excellent the individual.

The human case: Chapman's leaders didn't just perform better—they became more capable versions of themselves. Several eventually left to run other companies, taking developed capabilities to create value elsewhere. When asked about success, Chapman pointed not to revenue but to "how many people we've sent into the world more capable than when they arrived." Development wasn't a retention strategy. It was the point.

Your Fulfillment Reality Check

This process reveals something more practical than an emotional preference: It shows whether your instincts are building compound capability or limiting it to your personal capacity.

Think about the last five times you felt genuinely proud or satisfied at work. For each one, identify which category fits:

CATEGORY A: PERSONAL ACHIEVEMENT

- You personally solved a difficult problem.
- You made a critical decision that worked.
- Your expertise saved the situation.
- People recognized your individual contribution.

CATEGORY B: OTHERS' GROWTH

- Someone used a framework you taught them.
- A person you coached handled something independently.
- Your team executed well using your approach.
- Someone thanked you for developing their capability.

CATEGORY C: SYSTEM SUCCESS

- A breakthrough happened that you didn't personally drive.
- Someone solved a problem better than you would have.
- The team succeeded during your absence.
- People you developed are now developing others.

YOUR PATTERN

- Four to five in category A = Controller (satisfaction from being the hero)

- Three or more in category B = Builder (satisfaction from developing others)
- Three or more in category C = Architect (satisfaction from what works without you)

What this reveals: If your pattern skews heavily toward category A, you may be leaving value on the table—capability that could compound isn't being built. The business case and the human case both suffer.

If your pattern skews heavily toward category C with little representation in category B, you may have systems that work but people who feel like cogs rather than contributors. The math works, but the meaning doesn't.

The leaders who build organizations that last—and that people want to be part of—find ways to create all three. Not because they're more virtuous, but because they've discovered these outcomes reinforce each other. Building people *is* how you build capability. Building capability *is* how you build people.

The immediate move: This week, resist solving *one* problem you could easily solve. Instead, ask: "What would you try?" and wait for their full answer.

Notice two things: what happened to the problem, and what happened to the person. That's the integration in action.

The Room Alex Built

Four years into his Architect transformation, Alex experienced his own breakthrough. It didn't happen during a crisis.

It happened on a Tuesday afternoon, in a meeting he almost skipped.

ParagonCX's largest enterprise customer had been threatening contract termination over an integration challenge. Sarah had taken point. Alex had stepped back. By the time he wandered past the conference room—on his way to a different meeting entirely—Sarah was already deep into a war room session with engineering, sales, and product.

He paused at the glass wall. Watched.

Sarah was at the whiteboard, walking the team through a reframe Alex hadn't considered. "Instead of trying to build what they're asking for," she was saying, "what if we solve the underlying business problem using our existing capabilities?" She was using decision frameworks Alex had taught her—but she'd adapted them. Simplified the triage. Added a stakeholder lens he'd never built in. Made them *hers.*

Two hours later, she presented a solution that was better than anything he would have developed. Not marginally better. Architecturally better. The kind of solution that would have taken Alex three iterations to reach, and Sarah got there in one session because she wasn't defending her own past decisions the way he would have been.

Alex was back at his desk, halfway through an email, when he realized he'd stopped thinking about the customer problem. Not pushed it aside. Not forced himself to let go. He'd simply . . . forgotten to worry about it. His mind had moved on to a hiring strategy he'd been noodling over for weeks—the kind of long-horizon thinking that used to be impossible when every crisis demanded his hands.

He sat back in his chair.

When had that happened? When had he stopped tracking whether things would fall apart without him?

It wasn't relief. He knew what relief felt like—he'd felt it after Japan, after the RevenueCorp recovery, after every test his systems passed. This was different. This was the absence of something he'd carried so long he'd forgotten it was there. The low-grade vigilance. The background hum of *Is it working? Is it holding? Do they still need me?*

It was gone. And he hadn't noticed it leaving.

He thought about Bob Chapman's question—*What if success meant how many people you sent into the world more capable than when they arrived?* Alex had understood it intellectually for years. But sitting at his desk, not worrying about a crisis he didn't need to worry about, thinking instead about who to hire next and what they might build—he felt it for the first time as something true about himself. Not an aspiration. Not a principle. Just the way things were.

She's better at this than I ever was. And I'm not keeping score.

That was the part he hadn't expected. Not that they could succeed without him—he'd known that for a year. But that he'd stopped measuring his own value against their performance. That their success had become the source of his satisfaction, not a threat to it. Not because he'd decided it should be. Because it just . . . was.

For the first time in his career, Alex's fulfillment didn't depend on being the hero, the Architect, or even the Builder. It came from something quieter: The room was smarter than he was, and that felt like enough.

The Signal Box

True delegation transforms leadership from personal achievement into compound capability—for the business and for the people in it.

Key insights from this chapter:

- Building organizational capability creates compound value that individual heroics can never match—no matter how brilliant the individual.
- Chapman's breakthrough: Developing the best leaders for every situation builds both a more valuable company and more capable humans. These aren't separate outcomes.
- Some leaders find deep satisfaction in this shift; others simply recognize it's how great organizations get built. Both are valid reasons to make the move.
- The goal isn't working less—it's building something that serves more people more sustainably than individual heroics ever could.

When your team routinely achieves breakthroughs you couldn't have imagined, you've built a room that's smarter than you.

> **If you remember only one thing: When they stop needing you in the moment is the moment you've built something real.**

Learning Prompt

Here's something worth noticing: Some leaders get energized when their people succeed independently, while others feel threatened or unnecessary. Neither reaction determines whether you can make this shift—but understanding your reaction helps you design the transition.

Think about a time when someone you developed succeeded without your involvement. What happened to the outcome? What happened to them? What did you notice about yourself?

This week, identify one capability you could transfer that would simultaneously free you for higher-leverage work *and* develop someone else's capacity. Design the transfer as an experiment in building both.

The curiosity: You might discover that business value and people development aren't trade-offs to manage—they're the same investment paying returns in two currencies.

CHAPTER 12

Escaping the Hamster Wheel of Success

Building Systems That Run Without You

If it breaks when you leave, you never built it.

When the urgent consistently crowds out the significant, struggle or failure follows.

In 2021, Jeff Bezos made an announcement that demonstrated decades of systematic leadership: He would step down as CEO of Amazon to become executive chair, focusing on new products and early initiatives while allowing the systems he'd built to operate independently.

Most observers expected this transition to create challenges. After all, Bezos was the visionary who had built Amazon from a garage start-up to one of the world's most valuable companies, the strategist who had guided their expansion into cloud computing, and the leader who had established their famous culture of customer obsession.

Instead, something remarkable happened. Amazon's performance remained strong and its innovation accelerated.

The Architecture Behind Independence

What enabled this smooth transition wasn't luck. It was the systematic architecture that Bezos had been building for over two decades:

- **The leadership principles system:** Fourteen principles create ninety-one possible interaction combinations, enabling emergent behaviors that no single leader could direct.
- **Customer data architecture:** Real-time customer behavior patterns inform decisions across business units without requiring executive coordination.
- **Working backward process:** Innovation decisions start with customer benefit and work backward to solution, ensuring alignment without micromanagement.
- **Two-way-door decision framework:** Teams can make fast decisions on reversible choices while reserving irreversible decisions for careful deliberation.

The Systems Independence Test

The ultimate validation came not when Bezos stepped down, but in how Amazon had been operating for years before his transition. Business units were already making autonomous decisions that aligned with long-term strategy:

- **AWS innovation:** Cloud services emerged from internal needs becoming external opportunities. Intelligence emerging from system interaction rather than executive direction.
- **Prime development:** The subscription model evolved through customer feedback loops rather than top-down planning.
- **Marketplace expansion:** The third-party seller platform grew through a systematic response to customer needs rather than a centralized strategy.
- **International growth:** Regional teams made autonomous decisions based on local market intelligence while maintaining global coherence.

The Real Goal: Stop Looking Down, Start Looking Out

Bezos's systematic approach revealed something profound about leadership effectiveness: Why do you want systems that work without you?

> **The answer isn't efficiency. It's freedom.**

Freedom to stop looking down at the problems in front of you and start looking out at the possibilities ahead of you.

Controllers spend their time looking down:

- at problems to solve
- at fires to fight
- at decisions waiting for approval
- at processes that need their oversight

Architects learn to look out:

- at opportunities to create
- at systems to design
- at futures to build
- at possibilities others can't yet see

The ultimate goal of systematic leadership is simple: Fire yourself from the day to day so you can focus on designing and creating the future.

Your Sustainable Leadership Assessment

This is the final synthesis. You've assessed yourself across systems thinking, delegation, network architecture, strategic patience, and emotional fulfillment patterns. Now the question is integration: not where you are in any single domain, but whether your transformation holds when you're not actively managing it. The truest test of architectural leadership isn't what works when you're present—it's what keeps working when you're gone.

What this assessment reveals: How well your systems work when you're not there. This is different from uncertainty handling or delegation patterns.

Rate each statement by checking the column that best describes your current reality:

When you're absent from the organization:

- ✓ **Controller:** You check your phone constantly, knowing important decisions are piling up. When you return, you find projects stalled, team members waiting for your direction, and problems that spiral without your intervention. You feel both needed and trapped by this dependency.
- ✓ **Builder:** You've built some systems that continue working, but you still get "quick question" texts about complex challenges. Teams can handle routine operations but reach out when situations require judgment. You feel proud of their growth but aware they still need your frameworks.
- ✓ **Architect:** Your phone stays quiet during your absence. When you return, you find decisions were made, problems were solved, and work progressed without any decline in quality. You feel that rare satisfaction of building something that works better without you.

When measuring organizational independence:

- ✓ **Controller:** You track what gets accomplished when you're directly supervising versus when you're not. You notice the difference and feel responsible for maintaining constant involvement to ensure quality outcomes.
- ✓ **Builder:** You measure both immediate results and the capabilities you've built in others. You're excited to see frameworks being applied but notice teams still depend on your refinement of their application.
- ✓ **Architect:** You track autonomous excellence and compound capability development. You feel fulfilled watching

capabilities multiply through people you've developed, creating organizational intelligence that exceeds what you could generate personally.

When people achieve breakthrough results:

- ✓ **Controller:** You feel pride in outcomes you directly influenced through your involvement. You can trace your contribution to the success and feel valued for the role you played in making it happen.
- ✓ **Builder:** You feel satisfied seeing people apply frameworks and capabilities that you helped them develop. Their success validates your development approach, and you enjoy seeing your teaching multiplied through their application.
- ✓ **Architect:** You feel profound fulfillment when achievements exceed what you could have accomplished personally. When people create solutions you never would have imagined using principles you helped establish, you experience that rare joy of building something bigger than yourself.

When considering your leadership legacy:

- ✓ **Controller:** You want to be remembered for the important problems you personally solved and the critical decisions you made. Your legacy feels tied to your individual contributions and the direct impact you had on outcomes.
- ✓ **Builder:** You want to be remembered for the people you developed and the capabilities you built in others. Your legacy feels connected to the multiplication of your frameworks and approaches through people you taught.
- ✓ **Architect:** You want to be remembered for what works better because you were there, not while you were there. Your legacy feels tied to systems that enable innovations you never could have imagined, continuing to create value long after your involvement.

What Your Integration Pattern Reveals

Throughout this book, you've explored Controller → Builder → Architect patterns across systems thinking, membership design, delegation, network building, cross-functional fluency, stakeholder architecture, strategic patience, chaos comfort, and delegation mastery. Your assessment results reveal not just where you are in sustainable leadership, but how successfully you've integrated the entire architectural transformation.

If your assessment shows mostly Controller patterns: You're still carrying the organization on your back. This worked to get you here—it won't get you where you need to go. The hard truth: Reading about architectural leadership isn't the same as practicing it. You understand the concepts intellectually, but you haven't released hero identity behaviorally.

The good news: Every domain you systematize creates momentum for the next. Your breakthrough will come when you fully transform one high-impact area and experience what it feels like to build something that works without you. That experience, watching your systems create results while you're absent, breaks the addiction to indispensability more powerfully than any framework.

If your assessment shows mixed Controller/Builder patterns: You're in transition, but you may be stalling in the comfortable middle. You've proven you can build capabilities in others and create some systematic approaches. What you haven't proven yet is whether you can fully let go.

The danger zone: You stay involved as "the coach" or "the guide" because it feels like leadership, but it's hero behavior in Builder clothing. If teams still wait for your refinement of their application, if complex situations still require your judgment, if your frameworks only work when you're there to guide their use, you're not building architectural systems, you're building sophisticated dependency.

The pattern to watch: Are you coaching because people need development, or because you need to stay involved? If absence reveals that your systems don't work without your guidance, you've built Builder capabilities but not Architect systems.

If your assessment shows mostly Architect patterns: You've achieved what most leaders never do. You've built systems that work better without you. You've experienced that profound fulfillment of watching people create solutions you never imagined, using principles you established. You understand that sustainable leadership isn't about being needed; it's about building organizational intelligence that transcends individual limitations.

Your challenge isn't transformation anymore. It's replication and integration. Can you help other leaders make this transition? Can you teach architectural thinking, not just architectural systems? Can you create an organization where building systems that work without you becomes the cultural norm rather than the exception?

The ultimate test: Are you building Architects or just better Builders who still depend on your architectural vision?

From Nuclear Submarines to Streaming Giants to Start-Ups

The same architectural principles that enabled Netflix to thrive during Hastings's sabbatical, and Captain Marquet's submarine crew to operate without his constant direction, also transform smaller organizations. The scale differs, but the fundamental shift from heroic leadership to systematic capability building follows the same pattern.

Alex Chen's transformation at ParagonCX followed this same journey, culminating in his own moment of recognizing that sustainable leadership had been achieved.

Three weeks before his planned vacation to Italy, Alex's sustainable leadership systems faced their first real stress test. A major security vulnerability was discovered in their core platform, requiring immediate patches across all client implementations. Simultaneously, their biggest prospect requested an accelerated demo timeline that would require significant engineering resources.

Alex's old instincts tugged at him to cancel the vacation and personally coordinate the response. Instead, he watched his systems handle what should have been a crisis requiring heroic intervention.

The security patch was deployed using the incident response protocols Sarah had refined. The prospect demo was rescheduled through the frameworks Marco had developed for resource allocation conflicts. Daily stand-ups kept everyone aligned without Alex moderating every decision.

It worked. But more importantly, it worked without him having to prove it would work. Still, as his plane took off for Italy, Alex wondered what would await him upon his return.

Alex stood in his empty office at 6 p.m. on his first day back from three weeks in Italy. He ran his finger along his clean desk—no sticky notes, no urgent printouts scattered around. The silence felt surreal after years of walking into chaos.

His inbox showed twelve messages, all nonurgent. He scrolled through them twice, looking for the crisis that never came. The crisis backlog that should have accumulated during his absence simply didn't exist.

He'd expected to return to chaos. Instead, he'd returned to a company that had thrived without him.

The strangest part wasn't that everything had run smoothly. It was that several things had improved. The team had launched a new feature ahead of schedule. Customer satisfaction scores had increased. Two major partnership deals had closed—deals he would have insisted on handling personally just six months ago.

Alex walked down the hall to the engineering pod. Through the glass, he could see Marco leading a design review with the kind of strategic thinking that Alex used to believe only he possessed. In the customer success area, Sarah was training two new hires using frameworks she'd developed while he was gone.

When did they become so capable?

The answer arrived slowly, then all at once: They'd always been capable. He'd just never created space for them to prove it. The realization settled in his stomach—not disappointment, but something deeper. Relief mixed with pride mixed with a strange kind of grief for his old identity.

Alex returned to his office and opened his laptop. But instead of diving into the day-to-day issues that used to consume him, he found himself staring at a blank document titled "Future Strategic Opportunities."

For the first time in his career, Alex Chen had the cognitive freedom to think about problems that didn't exist yet. To design futures instead of fix presents. To look out instead of down.

He started typing: "What if we could predict customer churn not just for our clients, but for any B2B relationship? What if our AI could . . ."

Three hours later, Alex realized he'd been completely absorbed in possibility thinking. The kind of strategic work that had been impossible when he was trapped in operational heroics.

His phone buzzed with a text from Maya: "Welcome back! How does it feel to be irrelevant?"

Alex laughed, feeling the truth of it in his body—not the sting of rejection, but the satisfaction of building something bigger than himself. He typed back: "Like nothing I have felt before."

Two weeks later, Alex sat in the third row of the middle school auditorium, phone left in the car. He'd learned that trick three recitals ago—undivided attention meant undivided.

When Sophie walked onto the stage, her eyes swept over the audience. She found him on the first look.

Their eyes met. A quick smile passed between them.

Then she turned to face the judges. Alex felt something settle in his chest. Pride in his daughter. Pride in himself. And something quieter underneath—contentment. The kind that comes when you finally stop being the person you never wanted to become.

She was no longer looking to see if he was there. She was looking to see where his smiling eyes met hers.

Design becomes real only when it's practiced. To see how other leaders have built their systems, refer to appendix II, "Architect Systems in Practice" (access the appendices at *catalystgrowthadvisors.com/the-hero-trap/*). Each example—from Amazon's clarity to Zingerman's adaptability—shows how belief becomes structure. Use them as models when building your own system of performance.

The Ultimate Test

The vacation test reveals everything: where you've escaped the Hero Trap, where you're still stuck, and where your next architectural work must focus. But the ultimate test isn't a vacation—it's whether the organization thrives when you leave permanently.

Five years into Alex's Architect transformation, ParagonCX faced that test when Alex was recruited for a CEO role at a larger company.

Most successions fail because the departing leader was the system. Alex had spent two years ensuring he wasn't. Quarterly month-long sabbaticals revealed dependencies that got systematically eliminated. Multiple team members had been developed using the same architectural frameworks Alex had learned. The culture wasn't dependent on Alex's personality—it was embedded in systematic approaches to decision-making and problem-solving that worked regardless of who was leading.

Maya, who had progressed from VP of product to leading European operations using those frameworks, stepped into the CEO role. The transition took weeks, not months. The systems made it possible.

Results after Alex's departure: Revenue growth accelerated, decision-making got faster, and innovation increased as Maya's fresh perspective combined with the systematic approaches Alex had built. The culture held. The company thrived.

By the time Alex started his new role, ParagonCX was running without him.

That was the proof.

The Mathematics of Legacy

Hero leadership adds. Architect leadership multiplies.

Every problem you solve adds one point to the scoreboard. When you stop, everything stops with you. But every system you design, every person you develop, keeps producing results long after you've moved on.

Heroes create speed. Architects create momentum. And momentum compounds forever.

Design beats default. The same capacity that made you excellent at solving problems can make you excellent at building problem solvers.

Before: I'm valuable because I solve difficult problems. *Now:* I'm valuable because I develop others who solve problems I couldn't.

Before: My worth comes from being indispensable. *Now:* My legacy comes from building something that works better without me.

The paradigm shift is complete when your deepest satisfaction comes not from what you accomplished, but from what others achieve using principles you built.

For a systematic version of the independence assessment Alex used, see the Quarterly Independence Test in appendix I (access the appendices at catalystgrowthadvisors.com/the-hero-trap/*).*

The Signal Box

Sustainable leadership isn't just about building systems—it's about building systems that reinforce Architect identity instead of rewarding hero behavior.

Key insights from this chapter:

- Heroes make themselves indispensable; Architects make themselves irrelevant to operations.
- Systems beat heroics because sustainable architecture creates compound organizational capability.
- Your brain craves indispensability, but leadership fulfillment comes from building lasting independence.
- The goal isn't elimination of leadership—it's creation of distributed leadership capability.
- Sustainable systems create more value over time than individual heroics ever could.
- The ultimate test: Does your organization's culture make it easier to be an Architect or to be a hero?

If you remember only one thing: The vacation test reveals everything: what thrives without you, what survives, and what breaks.

Learning Prompt

Most leaders say they want to build systems that run without them, but few test whether they've succeeded. The gap between intention and reality often reveals what we're unconsciously holding onto.

This week, step back from one area where you think you've built sustainable systems. Don't manage, don't intervene, just observe what happens.

What continues working smoothly? What starts to break down? What do people wait for your input on that they theoretically could handle independently?

If someone asks for your input: Ask "What are you thinking?" and wait for their full answer.

If their thinking is sound, say: "Run with it." If it has gaps, ask one question that points toward what they're missing. If they genuinely lack the information or authority to decide, give them what they need. Note it as a system gap to fix.

You're testing whether your systems give people the context and capability to decide well without you.

The insight: The difference between what you think you've systematized and what works without you reveals exactly where your next architectural work needs to focus.

EPILOGUE

What Works Better Because You Were There?

The call came on a Tuesday morning, eighteen months after Alex Chen had left ParagonCX to become CEO of a larger company.

"Alex, I wanted to give you an update on something remarkable," said Maya, who had taken over as CEO after his departure. In the eighteen months since he left, ParagonCX had grown to over four hundred employees. "Remember that AI capability we always talked about building but never had time for—the one that could predict customer churn across industries, not just within our platform?"

Alex smiled. He remembered. One of those *someday* projects—strategically important but always pushed aside by more immediate fires.

"We built it," Maya continued. "And it's working better than we ever imagined."

"How?" he asked.

"The frameworks you built. The green–yellow–red decision system. The capability development approach. The way you taught us to share context and make decisions with clear escalation paths. The system you created for building systems—it gave us the architecture to innovate beyond what either of us envisioned."

Alex turned toward the window. His hands weren't clenched. His shoulders relaxed.

"Honestly?" Maya said. "It's better than what we would have created with you in the room."

Four years ago, those words would have felt like a gut punch.

Today, they felt like confirmation.

After they hung up, Alex sat in silence. His mind drifted back to that moment three years earlier—returning from Italy to find his office empty, his company calm, and no crises waiting for him. Italy proved that the systems worked without him. Maya's call proved that they could work beyond him.

That evening, Alex left the office at 5:30. His new company was three months into a complex integration—the kind of situation that would have consumed the old Alex around the clock. But he'd spent those three months building decision frameworks and developing his leadership team, not solving every problem himself.

The integration would work. Or it would surface problems they'd fix together. Either way, his presence at every meeting wasn't what would determine success.

That Sunday, Sophie asked if he wanted to hear something. She sat on the edge of her bed, guitar across her lap, and started to play. "It's a big yellow house . . ." Her voice filled the small room. A song about home she'd written herself. When she finished, she didn't ask what he thought. She just said, "I wanted you to hear it first."

Alex couldn't remember the last time he'd been someone's first call for something that mattered.

That was the transformation no quarterly report could capture.

Your Move

You stand at that same decision point.

You can continue optimizing for heroic leadership—solving problems personally, maintaining control, and staying indispensable. The path is comfortable and gratifying, but finite.

Or you can commit to architectural leadership—designing systems, developing capability, and creating value that compounds beyond your presence.

One makes you feel valuable. The other builds lasting value.

The question isn't whether you're capable of architectural leadership. It's whether you're willing to trade short-term indispensability for long-term impact.

Your tenure won't be measured by what you accomplished personally. It will be measured by what works better because you were there.

If you remember nothing else, remember this: **Leadership ROI comes from moving through C → B → A. Solve it once. Teach it once. Watch it grow.**

Your Next Step

You've learned to see the Controller → Builder → Architect progression. Now find out exactly where you stand.

The **CBA Leadership Assessment** diagnoses your current patterns across the domains covered in this book—delegation, decision-making, team development, and system design. In ten minutes, you'll know precisely where you're operating as an Architect, where you're still building, and where Controller patterns are holding you back.

Download the assessment at *catalystgrowthadvisors.com/cba-assessment-download-enter-email-here/*.

Continue the Work

This book is a starting point. If you want to go further—through a workshop with your team, a speaking engagement for your organization, or a CEO cohort where you'll work alongside other leaders making the same transition—I'd welcome the conversation. I enjoy working with humble, hungry learners who challenge the status quo.

Find me at *catalystgrowthadvisors.com*.

Access *The Hero Trap* appendices at *catalystgrowthadvisors.com/the-hero-trap/*.

ACKNOWLEDGMENTS

Thanks to Maggie and Julie for your patience with yet another book project, and for reminding me that the transformation I write about starts at home.

Thank you to Marshall Goldsmith, who not only wrote the foreword but has modeled what it means to move from hero to Architect in his own career.

Thank you to those who took the time to read this work and put their names behind it: Amy Edmondson, Jonah Berger, Dorie Clark, Peter Bregman, Alisa Cohn, Sally Helgesen, Morag Barrett, Erica Dhawan, Chester Elton, Todd Cherches, and Lisa Nirell.

A special thanks to Todd Cherches for introducing me to Ken Lizotte, who helped get this book published with a high-quality and mission-aligned organization like Berrett-Koehler.

Thank you to the early readers and reviewers whose feedback shaped this book, with particular gratitude to Bryan Gilpin, Jeff Palm, and Craig Palli, whose suggestions were vital to shaping the final version.

Thank you to my clients, whose real transformations inspired the composite journey of Alex Chen. You trusted me with your leadership challenges, taught me as much as I taught you, and proved that the shift from hero to Architect is possible.

Thank you to my peers in the 100COACHES community, who continue to challenge and sharpen my thinking.

Finally, thanks to my BK champions Neal Maillet and Jeevan Sivasubramaniam, and the team at Berrett-Koehler for believing in this book and the Performance Operating System series it launches.

And to the thought leaders, past and present, whose work forms the foundation of this book: W. Edwards Deming, Peter Senge, Daniel Kahneman, Jonathan Haidt, Robert Hogan, Amy Edmondson, Marcus Buckingham, David Rock, Chip and Dan Heath, Bob Chapman, L. David Marquet, and the many others cited in these pages. I stand on your shoulders.

And, finally, to Alan Mulally, who reached out, invited me into 100COACHES, and then showed me what "Working Together" actually looks like at scale with humility and grace. Without that call in the summer of 2020, this book wouldn't exist. I am forever in your debt.

NOTES

This book stands on the shoulders of the thinkers referenced here, integrating their insights into a coherent system leaders can apply directly. Wherever possible, the book points readers back to these original works for deeper exploration.

Introduction

1 Jamais Cascio et al., *Navigating the Age of Chaos: A Sense-Making Guide to a BANI World That Doesn't Make Sense* (Berrett-Koehler Publishers, 2025). Cascio originated the BANI framework in 2018 and first published it publicly in "Facing the Age of Chaos" (Medium, 2020).

2 Leonid Rozenblit and Frank Keil, "The Misunderstood Limits of Folk Science: An Illusion of Explanatory Depth," *Cognitive Science* 26, no. 5 (2002): 521–562.

3 Ruth Malan, "Conway's Law," *Trace in the Sand* (blog), February 13, 2008, https://ruthmalan.com/traceinthesand/conwayslaw.htm.

Chapter 1

1 Robert Hogan and Robert B. Kaiser, "What We Know About Leadership," *Review of General Psychology* 9, no. 2 (2005): 169–180; Mark van Vugt, Robert Hogan, and Robert B. Kaiser, "Leadership, Followership, and Evolution: Some Lessons from the Past," *American Psychologist* 63, no. 3 (2008): 182–196.

2 Marcus Buckingham, *Nine Lies About Work: A Freethinking Leader's Guide to the Real World* (Harvard Business Review Press, 2019).

3 L. David Marquet, *Turn the Ship Around!: A True Story of Turning Followers into Leaders* (Portfolio, 2012).

4 David Rock, "SCARF: A Brain-Based Model for Collaborating with and Influencing Others," *NeuroLeadership Journal* (2008).

Chapter 2

1 Dan Heath, *Upstream: The Quest to Solve Problems Before They Happen* (Avid Reader Press, 2020).

2 W. Edwards Deming, *Out of the Crisis* (MIT Press, 1986); W. Edwards Deming, *The New Economics for Industry, Government, Education* (MIT Press, 1993).

3 Daniel Kahneman, *Thinking, Fast and Slow* (Farrar, Straus and Giroux, 2011).

4 Heath, *Upstream.*

Chapter 3

1 L. David Marquet, *Turn the Ship Around!: A True Story of Turning Followers into Leaders* (Portfolio, 2012).

2 Muzafer Sherif et al., *The Robbers Cave Experiment: Intergroup Conflict and Cooperation* (Wesleyan University Press, 1961).

3 Jonathan Haidt, *The Righteous Mind: Why Good People Are Divided by Politics and Religion* (Pantheon Books, 2012).

4 Robert Hogan and Robert B. Kaiser, "What We Know About Leadership," *Review of General Psychology* 9, no. 2 (2005): 169–180

5 Marcus Buckingham, *Nine Lies About Work: A Freethinking Leader's Guide to the Real World* (Harvard Business Review Press, 2019).

6 Marquet, *Turn the Ship Around!*

Chapter 4

1 Jonathan Haidt, *The Righteous Mind: Why Good People Are Divided by Politics and Religion* (Pantheon Books, 2012).

2 MIT Center for Collective Intelligence, collective intelligence research, group problem-solving studies, technology-enhanced collaboration frameworks, 2018–2024.

3 Daryl J. Bem, "Self-Perception Theory," *Advances in Experimental Social Psychology*, vol. 6 (Academic Press, 1972): 1–62.

Chapter 5

1 Eric Schmidt et al., *Trillion Dollar Coach: The Leadership Playbook of Silicon Valley's Bill Campbell* (Harper Business, 2019).

2 Stanley McChrystal, *Team of Teams: New Rules of Engagement for a Complex World* (Portfolio, 2015).

Chapter 6

1 Reid Hoffman and Ben Casnocha, *The Start-up of You: Adapt to the Future, Invest in Yourself, and Transform Your Career* (Crown Business, 2012); Reid Hoffman, Chris Yeh, and Bill Gates, *Blitzscaling: The Lightning-Fast Path to Building Massively Valuable Companies* (Currency, 2018).

2 David Rock, "SCARF: A Brain-Based Model for Collaborating with and Influencing Others," *NeuroLeadership Journal* (2008).

3 Amy C. Edmondson, *The Fearless Organization: Creating Psychological Safety for Learning, Innovation, and Growth* (Wiley, 2019).

Chapter 7

1 Satya Nadella, *Hit Refresh: The Quest to Rediscover Microsoft's Soul and Imagine a Better Future for Everyone* (HarperBusiness, 2017).

Chapter 8

1 Jonathan Haidt, *The Righteous Mind: Why Good People Are Divided by Politics and Religion* (Pantheon Books, 2012).

2 Ford Motor Company, "Working Together" Leadership and Management System and Business Plan Review (BPR) methodology under Alan Mulally, 2006–2014, Harvard Business School Case Studies.

Chapter 9

1 Charles Duhigg, *The Power of Habit: Why We Do What We Do in Life and Business* (Random House, 2012).

2 Gary Keller and Jay Papasan, *The ONE Thing: The Surprisingly Simple Truth Behind Extraordinary Results* (Bard Press, 2013).

Chapter 11

1 Bob Chapman and Raj Sisodia, *Everybody Matters: The Extraordinary Power of Caring for Your People Like Family* (Portfolio, 2015).

BIBLIOGRAPHY

Ackoff, Russell L. *Systems Thinking for Curious Managers.* Triarchy Press, 2010.

Amabile, Teresa, and Steven Kramer. *The Progress Principle: Using Small Wins to Ignite Joy, Engagement, and Creativity at Work.* Harvard Business Review Press, 2011.

Bem, Daryl J. "Self-Perception Theory." *Advances in Experimental Social Psychology*, vol. 6. Academic Press, 1972: 1–62.

Buckingham, Marcus. *Nine Lies About Work: A Freethinking Leader's Guide to the Real World.* Harvard Business Review Press, 2019.

Buckingham, Marcus, and Curt Coffman. *First, Break All the Rules: What the World's Greatest Managers Do Differently.* Simon & Schuster, 1999.

Cascio, Jamais. "Facing the Age of Chaos." Institute for the Future, 2020.

Cascio, Jamais, Bob Johansen, and Angela F. Williams. *Navigating the Age of Chaos: A Sense-Making Guide to a BANI World That Doesn't Make Sense*. Berrett-Koehler Publishers, 2025.

Chapman, Bob, and Raj Sisodia. *Everybody Matters: The Extraordinary Power of Caring for Your People Like Family.* Portfolio, 2015.

Chouinard, Yvon. *Let My People Go Surfing: The Education of a Reluctant Businessman.* Penguin, 2005; rev. ed., 2016.

Collins, Jim. *Good to Great: Why Some Companies Make the Leap . . . and Others Don't.* HarperBusiness, 2001.

Crabtree, Greg. *Simple Numbers, Straight Talk, Big Profits!* Greenleaf Book Group, 2011.

Deci, Edward L., and Richard M. Ryan. *Self-Determination Theory: Basic Psychological Needs in Motivation, Development, and Wellness.* Guilford Press, 2017.

Deming, W. Edwards. *The New Economics for Industry, Government, Education.* MIT Press, 1993.

Deming, W. Edwards. *Out of the Crisis.* MIT Press, 1986.

Doerr, John. *Measure What Matters: How Google, Bono, and the Gates Foundation Rock the World with OKRs.* Portfolio, 2018.

Drucker, Peter F. *The Effective Executive.* Harper & Row, 1967.

Duhigg, Charles. *The Power of Habit: Why We Do What We Do in Life and Business.* Random House, 2012.

Duke, Annie. *Thinking in Bets: Making Smarter Decisions When You Don't Have All the Facts.* Portfolio, 2018.

Edmondson, Amy C. *The Fearless Organization: Creating Psychological Safety for Learning, Innovation, and Growth.* Wiley, 2019.

Flynn, Bill. *Further, Faster: The Vital Few Steps That Take the Guesswork Out of Growth.* Lioncrest Publishing, 2018.

Haidt, Jonathan. *The Righteous Mind: Why Good People Are Divided by Politics and Religion.* Pantheon Books, 2020.

Hammer, Michael, and James Champy. *Reengineering the Corporation: A Manifesto for Business Revolution.* Harper Business, 1993.

Hastings, Reed, and Erin Meyer. *No Rules Rules: Netflix and the Culture of Reinvention.* Penguin Press, 2020.

Heath, Chip, and Dan Heath. *Decisive: How to Make Better Choices in Life and Work.* Crown Business, 2013.

Heath, Chip, and Dan Heath. *Switch: How to Change Things When Change Is Hard.* Crown Business, 2010.

Heath, Dan. *Upstream: The Quest to Solve Problems Before They Happen.* Avid Reader Press, 2020.

Hoffman, Reid, and Ben Casnocha. *The Start-up of You: Adapt to the Future, Invest in Yourself, and Transform Your Career.* Crown Business, 2012.

Hoffman, Reid, Chris Yeh, and Bill Gates. *Blitzscaling: The Lightning-Fast Path to Building Massively Valuable Companies.* Currency, 2018.

Hogan, Robert, and Robert B. Kaiser. "What We Know About Leadership." *Review of General Psychology* 9, no. 2 (2005): 169–180.

Hubbard, Douglas. *How to Measure Anything: Finding the Value of Intangibles in Business.* Wiley, 2014.

Huselid, Mark A., Brian Becker, and Dave Ulrich. *The HR Scorecard: Linking People, Strategy, and Performance.* Harvard Business School Press, 2001.

Juran, Joseph M. *Juran on Leadership for Quality.* Free Press, 1989.

Kahneman, Daniel. *Thinking, Fast and Slow.* Farrar, Straus and Giroux, 2011.

Kahneman, Daniel, and Amos Tversky. "Judgment Under Uncertainty: Heuristics and Biases." *Science* 185, no. 4157 (1974): 1124–1131.

Keller, Gary, and Jay Papasan. *The ONE Thing: The Surprisingly Simple Truth Behind Extraordinary Results.* Bard Press, 2013.

Klein, Gary. *Sources of Power: How People Make Decisions.* MIT Press, 1998.

Kouzes, James, and Barry Posner. *The Leadership Challenge.* Jossey-Bass, 2017.

Lencioni, Patrick. *The Five Dysfunctions of a Team: A Leadership Fable.* Jossey-Bass, 2002.

Lieberman, Matthew D. *Social: Why Our Brains Are Wired to Connect.* Crown Publishers, 2013.

Marquet, L. David. *Turn the Ship Around!: A True Story of Turning Followers into Leaders.* Portfolio, 2012.

McChrystal, Stanley. *Team of Teams: New Rules of Engagement for a Complex World.* Portfolio, 2015.

Meadows, Donella H. *Thinking in Systems: A Primer.* Chelsea Green Publishing, 2008.

Michalowicz, Mike. *Profit First: Transform Your Business from a Cash-Eating Monster to a Money-Making Machine.* Portfolio, 2017.

Nadella, Satya. *Hit Refresh: The Quest to Rediscover Microsoft's Soul and Imagine a Better Future for Everyone.* HarperBusiness, 2017.

Ohno, Taiichi. *Toyota Production System: Beyond Large-Scale Production.* Productivity Press, 1988.

Pink, Daniel. *Drive: The Surprising Truth About What Motivates Us.* Riverhead Books, 2009.

Rock, David. "SCARF: A Brain-Based Model for Collaborating with and Influencing Others." *NeuroLeadership Journal* (2008).

Rozenblit, Leonid, and Frank Keil. "The Misunderstood Limits of Folk Science: An Illusion of Explanatory Depth." *Cognitive Science* 26 (2002): 521–562.

Rumelt, Richard. *Good Strategy Bad Strategy: The Difference and Why It Matters.* Crown Business, 2011.

Schmidt, Eric, Jonathan Rosenberg, and Alan Eagle. *Trillion Dollar Coach: The Leadership Playbook of Silicon Valley's Bill Campbell.* Harper Business, 2019.

Senge, Peter M. *The Fifth Discipline: The Art and Practice of the Learning Organization.* Doubleday, 1990.

Sherif, Muzafer, O. J. Harvey, B. Jack White, William R. Hood, and Carolyn W. Sherif. *The Robbers Cave Experiment: Intergroup Conflict and Cooperation.* Wesleyan University Press, 1961.

Spear, Steven J. *The High Velocity Edge: How Market Leaders Leverage Operational Excellence to Beat the Competition.* McGraw-Hill, 2009.

Stack, Jack. *The Great Game of Business: The Only Sensible Way to Run a Company.* Currency, 2013.

Sutherland, Jeff. *Scrum: The Art of Doing Twice the Work in Half the Time.* Currency, 2014.

Tetlock, Philip E. *Superforecasting: The Art and Science of Prediction.* Crown Publishers, 2015.

Van Vugt, Mark, Robert Hogan, and Robert B. Kaiser. "Leadership, Followership, and Evolution: Some Lessons from the Past." *American Psychologist* 63, no. 3 (2008): 182–196.

Wiseman, Liz. *Multipliers: How the Best Leaders Make Everyone Smarter.* Harper Business, 2010.

Womack, James P., and Daniel T. Jones. *Lean Thinking: Banish Waste and Create Wealth in Your Corporation.* Free Press, 2003.

INDEX

K

L

M

N

V

W

ABOUT THE AUTHOR

Bill Flynn spent thirty years trapped in his own success before he understood the problem.

As a VP of sales (eight times), CMO (twice), and GM, he built his career on being the person who fixed what others couldn't. Five successful exits, two IPOs, and seven acquisitions, including a turnaround during the 2008 financial crisis, all reinforced the same identity: He was valuable because he solved problems.

Then he became a coach. And he watched the same pattern limit leaders across every industry. Not because they were doing anything wrong, but because they were doing exactly what they'd been trained to do.

Over the past decade, Bill has coached hundreds of executives through the hero-to-Architect transformation. He is the author of *Further, Faster: The Vital Few Steps That Take the Guesswork Out of Growth*; is a member of Marshall Goldsmith's 100COACHES; and holds certifications from the NeuroLeadership Institute, Scaling Up, Gravitas Impact, and Predictive Index.

He wrote this book because awareness changes everything. Once you see the trap, you can choose your way out.

Berrett-Koehler
PUBLISHERS

Dear Reader,

Welcome to the Berrett-Koehler Community—a global network of changemakers creating positive impact in their lives, organizations, and communities.

Our Mission: Connecting People and Ideas to Create a World That Works for All

We believe transformation is possible. While outdated paradigms of self-interest, exclusion, and hierarchy continue to hold back our communities and organizations, we know that change can happen. That's why we connect people with actionable ideas from leading experts who are already creating the solutions we need.

The BK Way

We're an independent publisher that practices what we publish. Our books, digital resources, and community offerings provide practical pathways for building more just, equitable, and sustainable organizations and lives. Whether you're transforming your workplace, community, or personal practices, our publications meet you where you are with tools that work.

But we don't just talk about positive change—we live it. Through "The BK Way," we put stewardship and purpose before profit. As a benefit corporation, we're legally committed to benefiting all our stakeholders: authors, readers, employees, communities, and the environment.

As our gift to you, claim your free bestselling ebook at bkconnection.com/welcome. You'll also receive fresh leadership insights delivered to your inbox from bkconnection.com/blogs/the-bk-exchange.

You Make the Difference

We're grateful to our readers, authors, and community members, who bring our mission to life every day. Your stories of transformation inspire us and show others what's possible.

Share how BK publications are making a difference in your world at bkconnection.com/impact.

Your friends at Berrett-Koehler

Join the Berrett-Koehler Community

Are you passionate about supporting independent publishing and reading diverse voices and perspectives? Join the BK Community Membership Program and become a part of a vibrant literary community. To support mission-based publishing while saving up to 30 percent on all books and attending exclusive events, visit ideas .bkconnection.com/bkcommunity-join to learn more and become a member.

FSC www.fsc.org
MIX
Paper | Supporting responsible forestry
FSC® C005010